THE **49%** ARCHITECT, **51%** ENTREPRENEUR

THE

49%
ARCHITECT,
51%
ENTREPRENEUR

A BLUEPRINT FOR ENTREPRENEURSHIP IN ARCHITECTURE

EDGARD RIOS

Advantage | Books

Published by Advantage Books, Charleston, South Carolina.
An imprint of Advantage Media.

ADVANTAGE is a registered trademark, and the Advantage colophon is a trademark of Advantage Media Group, Inc.

Printed in the United States of America.

10 9 8 7 6 5 4 3 2 1

ISBN: 978-1-64225-815-8 (Paperback)
ISBN: 978-1-64225-814-1 (eBook)

LCCN: 2023909744

Cover design by Matthew Morse.
Layout design by Matthew Morse.

This publication is designed to provide accurate and authoritative information in regard to the subject matter covered. It is sold with the understanding that the publisher is not engaged in rendering legal, accounting, or other professional services. If legal advice or other expert assistance is required, the services of a competent professional person should be sought.

Advantage Books is an imprint of Advantage Media Group. Advantage Media helps busy entrepreneurs, CEOs, and leaders write and publish a book to grow their business and become the authority in their field. Advantage authors comprise an exclusive community of industry professionals, idea-makers, and thought leaders. For more information go to **advantagemedia.com**.

A VISION OF THE PATH TO SUCCESS IN ARCHITECTURE,
AND MY VISION FOR CITY PLANNING OF THE FUTURE.

For those who believe in themselves.
For those who do not leave things for tomorrow.
For those who discovered that "no" does not matter.
For those who want to transcend through architecture.
For those who always wanted to be architects.

TO MY WIFE

I met you one cold winter night, and ever since you've warmed my life.
Thank you for being my travel companion.

TO MY DAUGHTERS

My soul wouldn't be complete without having been a father.
From the moment you came into my life, I found something to fight for.
I learned that I could cry, but above all, I was taught to laugh.
You are the light in my eyes. Never change, but most importantly,
never let anyone tell you no.

Nothing on earth lasts forever: just a bit here.
Even jade smashes, gold breaks,
even the plumage of the quetzal tears.

—NEZAHUALCÓYOTL
SOVEREIGN CHICHIMECA OF TEXCOCO, 1450 AD
ARCHITECT & POET

AUTHOR'S NOTE

Quotes appearing throughout the book have been translated from the Spanish; occasionally, they will vary slightly from versions in English. In addition, some are from interviews in Spanish-language publications that may be less familiar to American readers.

The photos presented in this book are copyrighted to my firm. They represent some of the work we have done.

CONTENTS

ENTREPRENEURSHIP AND ARCHITECTURE

With the passage of time, people will not remember us for what we did for ourselves, but rather what we did for them, what we did for others, for our work, and for our architecture.

—EDGARD RIOS

Architecture is a form of leadership. Good architecture, that which endures, that which serves and does not serve itself, is that which will be remembered for the meaning that it had or has for the user. Architecture exists to serve mankind. The duty of our profession lies in providing spaces, be they single family, multifamily, or public spaces on small or larger scales, that substantially improve the interaction between people, that give more brightness and significance to each of them, and that help create a better environment.

ARCHITECTURE EXISTS TO SERVE MANKIND.

Think about Plaza San Marcos (Saint Mark's Square) in Venice and how that plaza, in the past and present, and surely the future, is a magnet for people as if time and space had not

1

elapsed. This plaza still evokes the fundamental creation of a wonderful canvas for the masterpieces of the Campanile, the Palacio Ducal, and the Basilica. The plaza and its buildings have been a gathering place of the people for centuries. The church offers a very important and sacred place for religion, and it is joined by the Doge's Palace and the Library Marciana as a cultural center, all this surrounded by vibrant commercial areas. All the important buildings work together to create a city center for their residents and to develop their culture around a single place.

The environments we design can create harmony between people. Our creations contribute to culture: for centuries, we architects have helped create the flavor of each region in which we interact, and the acceptance of our work by each community makes the works endure over time.

Another example is the Metropol Parasol, in Seville, Spain. This beautiful place has been transformed with the construction of a wooden roof, an impressive monument, 150 x 70 meters long with a height of twenty-six meters. It is an extraordinary example of architecture of two eras that collide to emerge as an icon for the city and to bring to the people of Seville a place to gather again.

Our increasingly chaotic cities are caused by poor urban planning, lack of resources, and haste in the execution of projects. This forces us to be more responsible in doing a good job with that little space that was borrowed, assigned, or entrusted to us by our clients. Here lies the leadership that we as architects assume by accepting that professional assignment. We are here on this planet to do something ... or simply to have something to do. What difference will we make? What will our legacy be? Having small- and low-budget project assignments does not take away the duty of completing a project with the highest level of professionalism.

We have wrongly designed our cities in the last one hundred years around the automobile, not the people. You can see this easily in places like Mexico City, Los Angeles, São Paulo, and almost all large cities, especially in developed countries … others are still struggling to grow, like many African cities, and worse, others have copied bad designs and planning around the automobile again, like Dubai.

Our cities are the sum of their parts, and we have an important role as leaders through our architecture. Let us be leaders of change then and leaders in our profession.

I feel the only desire that one can truly permit. Freedom: Asking for nothing. Not expecting anything. Not relying on anything.

—AYN RAND, *THE FOUNTAINHEAD*

How Entrepreneurship and Architecture Are Linked

Entrepreneurs and architects are often one and the same. They are both creators; sometimes both are leaders; sometimes both lose, but many times they win. However, the best of both always get up if they stumble. Both are influential to others, and sometimes both leave a mark forever.

Something indisputable is that they are entwined, as when two atoms come together and form a molecule. Entrepreneurship and architecture are usually intrinsically linked. The architecture molecule is in all of us. We live it day by day, we suffer it day by day, but through it we visualize the past and face the future as a society.

Why I Wrote This Book

I wrote this book to encourage a new way of thinking about our cities, to encourage young architects to become urbanists, to encourage people to think outside of the box, to forget about old trends, to skip listening to our politics and urban authorities, and to change from inside to start a chain reaction to help others one by one. I want to inspire all of us to grow change from our own selves, concentrating first on our own capacities, and then in a group working together and pursuing our goals.

I also want to inspire and to help us all to recognize that *urbanism* is a responsibility of all. But for this to happen, we need to be participants … not only observers.

Urbanism; noun

ur·ban·ism; **ur**-b*uh*-niz-*uhm*

1: the characteristic way of life of city dwellers
2: a: the study of the physical needs of urban societies
    b: city planning

I hope this book serves to raise awareness, from ordinary dwellers to the most influential architects, to move our cities to what's next, to recognize that all are created equal, and that our only differences sometimes come from the opportunity to be born in a "golden" cradle, versus those who dare to challenge their circumstances.

There are only two things that we can permanently lose: the first is life itself; the second is time. The first one is inevitable, but the second one is unforgivable.

It's time to move ahead with new urbanism; we have great architects and multiple examples of the best of architecture. However, architects work most of the time developing the best project for that single lot of land, without thinking of how to respect and mix their architecture with the surroundings. We need as architects and as society to be more inclusive, to think about the whole and not only about our individualism.

I really hope this book can light the path for young people about to become architects, to help discover new heroes in the brilliant careers of Frank Lloyd Wright, Le Corbusier, Pelli, Tange, Bernini, Gaudi, Eiffel, Mies van der Rohe, Niemeyer, Hadid, Barragán, and many more to come, especially that young student who from their heart embraces this beautiful profession and one day will be the hero or heroine of others.

CHAPTER ONE

LIFE LESSONS FOR THE ARCHITECT/ ENTREPRENEUR

FACING FEARS AND MOVING FORWARD

The worst that can happen is being told no.

—RICARDO RÍOS, MY FATHER

When we stand at certain points in our lives, we can look behind us and see the moments that helped contribute to our chosen paths.

It's those small childhood learnings, those little life lessons that throughout our existence mark us forever. Some quirky details, some strong lessons, but that compendium of *c'est la vie* forges our character, for better or for worse.

Life is 10 percent what happens to you
and 90 percent how you react to it.

—CHARLES R. SWINDOLL

For some of us, architecture appreciation also starts as a vibrant memory, the first tall building we visited, the first modern stadium, or perhaps the first time we traveled to different places and cultures. Your first glimpse of the life of an entrepreneur may have been the first time you sold one of your toys at a garage sale ... and then discovered that you could now purchase a new one with the money earned.

Another lesson we learn that we carry with us as we move through our lives and careers is how to face the word "no." For me, it is a fuel I discovered I have in my veins, a fuel I use again and again as I learn to transform negative into positive.

I remember it as if it were yesterday, the place, my tennis club, the last frontier, in the southern part of my beloved Mexico, home to excellent memories, heat, rain, humidity that drowns, and friendships that refresh.

She was sixteen, and I was fourteen. It is the age of awakening to everything, the age of *I can do everything*, the age when I found the strength to tell the woman of my dreams that ... *what do I say? How do I start?* My first and best coach, my father, gave me my first life lesson.

"My son, the worst that can happen is she says 'no.'"

The setting: a New Year's Eve party at my club, ten at night. She was with her friends, all her age (yes, older, but what does it matter if love does not recognize age or any condition?). I approached her alone; I had no wingman, or rather, wing *boy*. I said, "Hi, can you come with me? I want to talk to you." I took her hand in mine, and we walked toward the swings. Thirty steps felt like an eternity, especially with the astonished glances of her friends and mine, each group in its own corner. Courage turned into seven words: "Do you want to be my girlfriend?"

Silence.

Eternal silence, sweet eyes … then, "Thank you, how cute, but you're very young." Thirty steps back, but not more than a thousandth of a second after her answer: light, peace. It reminds me of the day I paraglided in Valle de Bravo. Before the jump there was only fear and nerves, but a thousandth of a second after the act, an unexpected feeling of peace and tranquility came over me.

The lesson: it's true (thanks, Dad). Yes, there is light in the dark. Nothing really happened, that *no*, on the contrary, guided my days to date, since I discovered that, in fact, I was still alive, and even felt somewhat liberated. Thanks to that, I learned not to tell myself *no*, to face any circumstance, and if the *no* was to appear again, I would know how to turn it around and achieve the *yes* in all my objectives.

In that moment, I was a hero to my friends. "How could you do it? Admirable!" Of course, along with other adjectives I don't want to mention. The *no* created in me a security that I have not lost.

Face your fears and do it anyway!

Life throws challenges at us at every moment, some simple and others difficult, but the first line of battle is fought with ourselves. Never say no to yourself, and you've already won half the battle.

As an architect, student, or professional, you will meet the word "no" often, so learn from that and transform it into yes—maybe a better project, a better job—to take that opportunity that awaits you, maybe in a different city or in a different country. Life is about the risks we take.

Imagine Gustave Eiffel presenting the Eiffel Tower for the first time; it will be the first time a building that tall will be produced, the first time any construction like the Tower will be erected. Imagine he has a watch in his hand, because the World Exposition will be in Paris in two years to come. He was unafraid to innovate and challenge himself and the world of architecture.

Tennis is my passion, and in that sport, your serve is 50 percent of the battle. Master your serve and you will have half the game under control. There will be many times when you will hear the naysayers, those who want you to fail and not achieve your goals, and they will try to pull you to their side. Resist and instead use them as a source of energy to get closer to the *yes*.

As in tennis, the stronger I get served, the stronger I return it. Action and reaction.

CHAPTER TWO

TIME AND INSPIRATION

OUR MOST PRECIOUS COMMODITIES

Do not leave for tomorrow what you can do today.

—CARY CASTELLANOS DE RÍOS, MY MOTHER

Time is the good that has no replacement. Once it is gone, it can never return.

I learned many things from my parents. The example that both set formed me day by day, and those little teachings from my mother, such as "do not leave for tomorrow what you can do today," still haunt me in my daily work. This command in my ear has served me mainly to get what I dislike out

> **TIME IS THE GOOD THAT HAS NO REPLACEMENT. ONCE IT IS GONE, IT CAN NEVER RETURN.**

11

of the way as quickly as possible, freeing up a huge amount of free time to enjoy or do what I do find attractive.

In these modern times, we have extremely efficient technological distractors, efficient at least in principle. The television that came to capture our valuable time is now reaffirmed by the streaming services that we can enjoy either on the television itself or on our own smart devices. Worse yet … the blessed smartphones went from being valuable communication facilitators to being humanity's favorite toy—responsible for the real *walking dead*. I insist, *time* is given to us only once, and why then not invest it in the best possible way? Why not take advantage of it?

THE BEST TIME IS NOW, NOT TOMORROW. THE FASTEST ACTION OFFERS UNIMAGINABLE ADVANTAGES. THE WORLD BELONGS TO THOSE WHO MOVE FASTER.

I learned from my mother that the best time is now, not tomorrow, and that the fastest action offers unimaginable advantages. The world belongs to those who move faster.

I once read that there are two types of time, that of the clock and that of the mind. The former has sixty seconds for every minute, and every hour, in turn, has sixty minutes until it reaches twenty-four hours, then the cycle starts all over again. The second type of time, that of the mind, is the one we create ourselves, the one we can modify to our liking, since it is personal to each and every one of us. The important thing for both is to take advantage of them in the most efficient way and with discipline. When I design, I am lost in time; hours can pass, and I am still so involved in that which I am passionate about that I don't *feel* the hours pass. But don't ask me to queue at the bank because I'll get desperate after just a few seconds.

If you have a well-defined action plan, the time you dedicate to that which you are doing will always be well spent. It is very important to start each day by taking the time to organize your activities and specific goals, to establish for each day that *one thing* … the most important goal to achieve on that day.

The most precious resource we all have is time.

—STEVE JOBS

Authentic Urbanism and Time

Authentic urbanism is built over time. That's the main difference versus individual architecture projects. The time frame is short for individual projects, and for urbanism the timeline is long and based on the changing necessities of the people or the economy and cultural development of his citizens.

Let's take Brasilia, the federal capital of Brazil, as an example. Once Lúcio Costa, the city's urban designer wrote, "Don't bother visiting Brasilia if you've already formed an opinion and have preconceived ideas." The city is a miracle in its own right, built at a record speed between 1956 and 1961. It's a city full of sculptural, magnificent architecture mainly designed by Oscar Niemeyer, a genius who once worked with Le Corbusier.

Brasilia is facing many of the problems of most cities. Those with power live in glass bubbles, and those without power live in large apartment complexes or outside the city; the city has become a mirror of their society.

Time is the most valuable thing a person can spend.

—THEOPHRASTUS, GREEK PHILOSOPHER

Architecture Careers, Goals, and Time

Building a career as an architect takes a lot of time (a good type of time spent), so start looking for what you like first and what you love second. This means that you need to work with different types of architectural firms when starting out. This is not a path that can be skipped if you really want to become a great architect. Think of architecture as the long game. Visualize yourself in five, ten, and fifteen years. Time will fly as you immerse yourself in your chosen career. My personal recommendation is to work twelve to eighteen months in different firms or different classes of projects; don't stagnate in one type at first until you discover your true love.

Your first goal should also be to find a mentor, an outsider, or a senior architect who can clarify your goals and help you focus on them.

The best goals are those that are written down, those that can be revisited and measured. They are ideas of an instant that, if you don't catch, you lose forever.

On countless occasions we are presented with the opportunity to listen to talks or presentations from people with very valuable experiences, whether in a university presentation, a lecture, from a conversation with a mentor, etc. When listening to them, in that small instant the "light" in our imagination is turned on through the spark of the speaker. It is, therefore, of utmost importance to have the good practice of writing down valuable ideas, plans, or project ideas at those moments of inspiration.

The *why* is very simple. The exercise of our daily and repetitive activities robs us of time for what is really important. They distract us and perhaps are the reason we forget that great idea. We all come up with great ideas, but jumping from idea to practice, from practice to development, and finally to reaching that goal, is an objective that very few achieve. This simple habit of writing down our inspirations and ideas can make the difference between starting something or losing it forever.

To write an idea is similar to a famous sketch on a napkin, one which changed how the world thought about architecture. The Crystal Palace of Hyde Park in 1851 was a wonder of the Victorian era, the largest building for that time. Joseph Paxton, an experienced gardener at Chatsworth House, appeared with the brilliant idea on a napkin paper. Track your ideas no matter how simple they might seem.

An entrepreneur catches the idea and maximizes it over time, through an exercise of trial and error. As the saying goes: he who perseveres, reaches. Prioritize, organize, and execute your activities, seeking to maximize time for what really motivates, ignites passion, and inspires you. Entrepreneurs are individuals who transform their ideas into fully operational businesses. Most of the time, these are individuals who find opportunities throughout their daily lives. Architects work with the same philosophy. When we are asked to design a type of building or project to meet the needs of our clients, we analyze their needs, we delve into the operation of each of the users, we compare similar solutions, and we adapt our ideas and experiences to develop the best possible project within the parameters of cost, time, functionality, and customer needs.

At some point in my architecture career, I heard somewhere that the designer of the majestic Sydney Opera House came up with the idea while sipping coffee at a café, and in order not to lose it, he too drew it on his napkin.

Holding Fast to Our Ideas

During our professional development, we will meet with detractors of talent, envious people. At different stages of our lives, we will encounter various obstacles. We should be open to criticism and new ideas, but we should also hold fast to our ideas. It is very important to know how to manage our emotional intelligence. We should not let our reactions to others' opinions distract us from our talent. Learn to listen to that quiet voice inside that tells you when you are on the right track.

In our professional development, whether it be architecture or not, on multiple occasions we will come across comments such as, "It looks very similar to …" or "How unoriginal!" Or, simply, "I don't like it." Well, all this we can use for professional growth, and I believe we learn much more from negative comments than from positive ones. You learn more from failure than from victory, although sometimes we are predisposed to fall into the same hole on more than one occasion. However, in the end, you also need to develop confidence in your vision.

Adapting to Change

We are living in complicated times of exponential change, especially all these changes generated and fired at us at fast paces by one of the evils of the twenty-first century, COVID-19. While we lived in the solitude of quarantine, being in the company of our inner selves now more than ever, many of us decided to find a balance between our lives and actions. Many of us rediscovered ourselves and adapted to these new changes.

Disease has often driven change in many professions and human behavior, and architecture doesn't escape that. Remember how, during COVID-19, we closed all interior spaces, how we used the elevators instead of touching stair rails, and how we started working from home, in turn envisioning new spaces needed in order to do so. As a result, many of us now will continue to work from home, at least in a hybrid fashion, instead of using an office. Real estate will have to adapt those spaces to new uses. During these unprecedented times, every type of public building suffered change, and office spaces worldwide fell into disuse.

In addition, the Great Resignation (or Great Reprioritization, as some call it) appears to be driving more change to every profession and their spaces. The spaces will need to change, and this is a great opportunity for entrepreneurial-driven architects.

Many of us generated valuable ideas during these times, driven by free time at home. Perhaps many of us will carry those ideas further, but for that to happen, it is important to catch them and hold them close, making them our own until they become a reality.

It is not the strongest of the species that survives,
but the one that adapts the fastest to change.

—CHARLES DARWIN

Know Your Why

Philosophers from Kierkegaard to Viktor Frankl to Simon Sinek (author of *Start with Why*) have examined human motivation and our "why." Why do we pursue our passions? What drives us in our pursuits? To tell the truth, few know their destiny in life, that *why* that Simon Sinek mentions. And even if we took identical twins who were given the same education and almost

IT IS UNDENIABLE TO ACCEPT THAT THE HOW, THE WHAT, OUR LIFE EXPERIENCES, AND THE INFLUENCE OF FAMILY GRADUALLY FORM US.

the same life experiences, it is certain that each one would find their destiny in a very different way.

It is undeniable to accept that the *how*, the *what*, our life experiences, and the influence of our parents and family nucleus (initially mentors, friends, and the social environment) are gradually forming us, like the sculptors of mud that from water and earth give shape through their hands to that creative idea and turn it into something new, all this as they turn their pottery wheel.

Tell me who your friends are, and I'll tell you who you are.

—ANCIENT PROVERB

CHAPTER THREE

MORE ENTREPRENEUR THAN ARCHITECT

THE CHALLENGES AND THRILLS OF ENTREPRENEURSHIP

Considered one of the branches of art, architecture has accompanied us in the development of civilizations, from the time of the first refuges created through the gestation of hunter-gatherer camps on to permanent structures. From the beginning, shelter and security, as the predominant needs and construction in primitive societies, have been the main elements of spatial organization.

The etymology that gives rise to the word "architecture" is the marriage of two Greek words *arkhi* and *tekton*, *arkhi* meaning chief and *tekton*, creator. In other words, an architect is the chief creator. This will drive my engineer friends crazy. The eternal dispute: who is the boss of whom? The architect or the engineer? Now that we have clarified the problem, let's continue with our topic. According to its theoretical definition, architecture is the art and the technique of designing, building, and modifying the human habitat. In short, and especially since the beginning of our existence, the architect has been an entrepreneur, a person who identifies opportunities within his or her professional field or interest and the organization of the resources necessary to achieve the development of a proposal.

It is a profession that teaches us to think like other professionals. Every time we are included in a project, we have to transform ourselves into that "character" who will use or inhabit the space. Who said all actors are on Broadway?

Today, the current architect, and even more so the future architect, needs to be more *entrepreneur* than *architect* since the fast pace of our society and the challenges we face on a daily basis require professionals who are constantly innovating and reengineering, not only to survive, but to adapt, to stand out, and to leave their legacy to an entire generation.

A profession is that which gives us a degree; a professional is someone who develops in an ethical manner, someone who develops within their profession in the best possible way and provides a solution beyond the client's requirements. I believe, without a doubt, that we are part of a highly demanding profession that leads us to be entrepreneurs day by day. It pushes us to innovate, solve, manage, and integrate work teams, becoming leader architects and entrepreneurs for each assigned project.

Some colleagues, organizations, and/or architectural firms are more innovative and have greater influence and better results in their works, in their professional practice, or in their profits than others … perhaps because of the entrepreneur that their leader is on the inside, that entrepreneur who is capable of transmitting that essence to the entire organization, and as a result, takes it one step higher.

Some are lone wolves, others come in tandem, teaming up with one or more partners. Everyone forms their career in different ways. External influences shape us as projects, clients, and assignments unfold. There are challenges or opportunities that we discover as our day-to-day career progresses, and it is important to have the ability to decipher which ones will take us to the next level and which ones will only be a distraction. As I have heard: "Fire 20 percent of your clients; they are absorbing 80 percent of your time, and you are neglecting the most valuable ones."

In my professional experience, I ascended very quickly and at an early age to an important step in the development of my architecture, but I got lost two or three times along the way. I almost broke at other points, but all my experiences were life lessons, and I discovered that not losing sight of the main goal, that which each of us carries within, somehow allowed me to keep going on in each and every occasion. As

DEVELOP WAYS TO CREATE MORE VALUE TO CUSTOMERS AND VALIDATE THOSE IDEAS EVERY OCCASION YOU HAVE.

entrepreneurs, we are also headstrong fools sometimes, and perhaps the biggest mistake we make is we believe way too much in ourselves. We want to go through walls that are not always passable.

In my case, my biggest problems were those difficult clients, those that consume 80 percent of your working time and represent less than 20 percent in revenue, so it's important to learn to say *no*. These clients distract you from what's important—the good clients—and the ones that respect your architecture and support you through the design and/or construction phases. So, learn to fire some of your clients.

As entrepreneurs, either as individuals or in teams, try to discover new windows of light, discover new doors to pass through, and develop a better you and a better team. Develop ways to create more value to customers and validate those ideas every occasion you have.

Great entrepreneurs come from all corners of life. There is no single profile or type of entrepreneur, but they have some characteristics in common.

- Curiosity
- Adaptability
- Confidence to stand by their decisions
- The ability to adapt quickly to changing situations
- Tolerance to risk
- The ability to learn from failure
- Innovation
- Persistence!

Life is full of surprises, so buckle up and enjoy the journey.

The Risks and Thrills of the Future

One of the thrills—and risks—of this era involves data and AI. Today, we are immersed on the internet, where information is handled daily and in large quantities with Big Data systems. Just twenty or thirty years ago, it was unthinkable to synthesize so much information in seconds. The speeds at which we can access and process information today is the stuff of science fiction. And to make the picture even more interesting, artificial intelligence (AI) is challenging humanity once again. Better and faster … I love a great challenge.

According to experts, there are two futures for the architecture profession, and both rest on technology. In the first, architects use technology to accelerate traditional ways of working. This is already happening and very quickly. In the second, technology not only optimizes or speeds up daily work but also displaces professional work. This means machines or systems capable of operating alone or with new users who need to have different skills from the architect of today will appear, and we will have to evolve.

There are species that evolved at great speeds and have adapted to changing circumstances, always mutating. In Nicaragua, there is a freshwater fish named *Ciclido Nicaraguensis*, and in just a hundred years, part of this species has divided into two subspecies, one with thin lips and another with thick ones, allowing it to feed on sharp rocks without injury, thus overcoming the new circumstances of its environment.

Similarly, we will have to evolve quickly if we hope to keep pace with technology. An example of artificial intelligence based on a design system and regenerative architecture is software that allows the architect to create a solution to a design problem through limitations and objectives that the architect or team establishes. This software plays a participatory and active role in the invention of the form. Let's go back to one of our first debates in architecture school: *Form versus function.* The eternal battle of which comes first—the architectural version of the chicken and the egg. Personally, I've always defended that *function* dominates form. Architecture is at the service of man, and thus, if it does not work, it isn't of use. If it were the form that dominated the function, a pot could be a house (of course, if we could fit).

In short, artificial intelligence systems will create 100 percent efficient spaces for a certain activity or use, for example, a hospital. AI can also shape those select spaces, possibly or very likely in the style of the architectural genius we choose, at unprecedented speed and with almost limitless options.

Architecture will surely evolve in these times of AI, becoming divided into two or three different areas. The first will be 100 percent technified, based on AI and architectural programmers, something like today's pilots, who only review the checklist before the flight, but everything else is almost fully automated. Within this stage there will be specialized "pilots." A vital point of this subspecialization is humanity's goals, such as achieving carbon zero cities, as established in the 2016 Paris Agreement, the goal of achieving more sustainable buildings and to be free of carbon emissions. The fight to reverse climate change will bring new opportunities to our sector, and AI will support achieving these goals in a more efficient manner.

AI CHALLENGES US ... OR RATHER, IT COMPLEMENTS US. IT WILL BE THERE TO SERVE ARCHITECTURE AND NOT TO BE SERVED BY IT.

The second division of our specialization will be becoming "artisan workshops" of unique architecture. Like the artist who is acclaimed for his paintings, these colleagues who manage to sneak through this door will be protected by their ingenuity and will be well paid by sophisticated clients.

The third division in the future will lead architecture to the creation of new underground, or even above-ground spaces. These architects will specialize in the highly technical work of designing suborbital stations and/or bases on other planets or satellites like the moon. Through these new ways of seeing our cities and our future, this subspecialty of architectural and urban preservation will utilize our eyes as the evaluators of what to preserve as new cities transform.

AI challenges us … or rather, it complements us. It will be there to serve architecture and not to be served by it.

Let's try to evolve along with technology, as the great masters of architecture of yesterday had to endure for centuries the challenging moments they had to live through.

CHAPTER FOUR

ENTREPRENEURS OF ARCHITECTURE

LEARNING FROM VISIONARIES

Simplicity is the ultimate sophistication.

—LEONARDO DA VINCI

Since the first civilizations were created, entrepreneurs and architects have existed. Perhaps the first ones had the idea to build something more durable to protect the tribe from the elements and enemies, the selection by proof and error of the ideal materials to do so, the leadership to organize the tribe to work toward certain goals. We as a profession have been leaving traces of our ideas as we build everywhere across the globe, from Machu Picchu to the Great Wall, from Giza to Teotihuacan, every civilization we can discover has left buildings that reflect their beliefs, their customs, their culture.

Our forebears discovered geometry and used that in architecture. They made earthen mounds, stone circles, megaliths, and enormous structures that surprise us today. No matter that many of these wonders have disappeared, we still marvel over their ingenuity today. Think about the pyramids, these mortar-free stone joineries used chiseled stones to create their shape. Additionally, the Egyptians used hieroglyphics, carvings, and bright frescoes on the rocks to create a statement. Similar ideas were part of the world of the Maya people, and many other civilizations that have left a legacy of their existence.

Thus, history and architecture have been hand in hand from the beginning of time. Through this process, advances have been made to the technology of construction, from the first mixes to combine rocks, to the baking of bricks, to the discovery of better foundations. We learned how to bring water from far away, to discover how to cut rock that will become granite. All these discoveries and improvements required the imagination of architects and the leadership of entrepreneurs, working together to create places for humans to live and work.

But we are still evolving as a civilization, so the path is open. We look to the future—but let's also look at some of the greats who came before us.

God is in the details.

– LUDWIG MIES VAN DER ROHE

Ludwig Mies van der Rohe

Ludwig Mies van der Rohe was a German-American architect who started working with his father in a quarry workshop. In 1905, he moved to Berlin, where he met Walter Gropius and Le Corbusier, who, along with Frank Lloyd Wright, are considered some of the greatest architects of the twentieth century.

Initially he was oriented toward neoclassical architecture, but a trip to the Netherlands led him to a change in interest, influenced by the Dutch urban planner Hendrik Petrus Berlage.

Life experiences, trips, mentors, and experiences; these move the spirits of men and women and undoubtedly more so those of architects and entrepreneurs. We are what we experience, and we transmit those experiences through our architecture.

Mies van der Rohe had the terrible luck, like all his contemporaries, of experiencing the First World War in 1914, the Spanish Flu pandemic from 1918 to 1920, the Great Depression, and the Second World War. Despite all that, he managed to overcome and continued to fight for his goals and ideals.

Among his extraordinary projects, the Seagram building in New York, in collaboration with Philip Johnson, stands out. This project would become a benchmark and symbol of the contemporary industrial world of the time, completed in 1958. Also, among hundreds of other projects, he made the German pavilion at the Barcelona International Exhibition in 1929, and the Crown Hall for the College of Architecture at the Illinois Institute of Technology, changing the standards of architecture in the use of steel and glass.

WE NEED TO REENGINEER OURSELVES FIRST, SUBSEQUENTLY OUR COMPANIES, OUR ENVIRONMENT, AND OUR WORLD.

Today we face the remnants of the COVID-19 pandemic—but it will surely not be our last. So, do we complain? Or do we take the opportunity to rediscover ourselves during this new normalcy? And not only that, but also to become better human beings by becoming resilient in the face of situations that we cannot control. We need to reengineer ourselves first, subsequently our companies, our environment, and our world and, like Mies did, fight for our goals and ideals.

Let us remember that architecture is the expression of society and the circumstances of its times. Projects or artistic works often reflect that influence of the epoch lived.

Architecture is deemed complete only upon the intervention of the human being who experiences it.

—TADAO ANDO

Tadao Ando

The great architect Tadao Ando was born a twin and separated at an early age from his brother. Tadao went to live with his grandmother, who instilled in him the talent for crafts. Life took him on many paths. For example, he boxed and traveled the world. Being a self-taught man, he was influenced like many of us by the great architecture of the early twentieth century. The great Le Corbusier, an icon of Franco-Swiss architecture who was ahead of his time, influenced him remarkably.

Perhaps many of us dream of architectural greatness, of winning a Pritzker, architecture's highest honor, of being recognized, but great architecture requires great mentors, that is, patrons who pay for our dreams. Very few succeed, and others may not have wanted to pay the price. For some, like Howard Roark in *The Fountainhead*, we did not want to lose our freedom.

In truth, it does not matter the size of the project you have to carry out, we all have the opportunity to make a great project from a small task. We can create a work that pleases its owners in the first instance and that respects the environment, as well as improves the visual appearance of the street, neighborhood, or region where it was built as much as possible.

Such was the influence of the master Le Corbusier on Ando, so much so that Ando named his dog Corbusier in tribute. I do not know if the master would have liked this, but that is another story. Tadao Ando, without a university education and without the practice of having worked for a master, began to design buildings. He simply and effectively followed his dreams. He went on to that stage that few dare.

Whenever we dream of something, in this case starting our own architecture firm, that first stage is the dream, the wanting. Many people get trapped here, and they do not go beyond the simple dream. They have no practical plan, just the idea, or the spark.

The second stage is formal planning. This is the business plan that is born from a deep evaluation of the *what,* which is turned into the *how.* We would not be jumping off the cliff without knowing what lies below and what the best way to go splash down safely is. Here remain many others, perhaps the dream was not so great, perhaps they did not allocate the necessary time, or perhaps the fear of failure was greater.

Finally, the third stage is execution.

For Tadao, that was daring to open his own firm, to forget about boxing and jump into architecture. Daring in terms of entrepreneurship, every time that we choose to undertake a goal, the more information we have, the better. Data from the Bureau of Labor Statistics shows that approximately "20 percent of new businesses fail during the first two years of being open; 45 percent during the first five years; and 65 percent fail during the first ten years. Only 25 percent make it to fifteen years or more."[1] Not bad. If we like betting, nearly 50/50 after five years sounds reasonable. This data is general for any type of company.

---

1   Michael T. Deane, "Top Six Reasons New Businesses Fail," December 30, 2022, https://www.investopedia.com/financial-edge/1010/top-6-reasons-new-businesses-fail.aspx#:~:text=Data%20from%20the%20BLS%20shows,to%2015%20years%20or%20more.

In architecture practice, the elements that are important to success include maintaining a close relationship with customers, providing additional services of value, and, of course, the quality of the design. If we look at the statistics for architectural firms only, the American Institute for Architects released a 2016 report that indicates 77.3 percent of firms have nine or fewer employees, representing one-fifth of all architects and billing 15.4 percent of the entire market in the United States. Half of the firms no longer exist after the fifth year, and 70 percent disappear by the tenth.

But returning to the remarkable career of master Ando, among the works that led to him being awarded the Pritzker in 1995, and which made his firm famous today and forever, are the Hyogo Prefectural Museum of Art in Kobe, Japan; the Hill of the Buddha in Sapporo, Japan; the restoration of the Punta della Dogana in Venice, Italy; and the formidable and simple Church of the Light in Ibaraki, Japan.

His architecture recognizes a double influence between rigid Japanese tradition and modernism. His buildings and designs provide simple, and at the same time, masterful, geometric vision. He uses traditional materials, such as concrete, but leaves them bare, as well as the harnessing and handling of natural light. His hallmark is the use of smooth concrete (apparent concrete), the material that is present in almost all his works. A self-taught person, he took his work to the next level.

> *There is a powerful need for symbolism, and that*
> *means the architecture must have something*
> *that appeals to the human heart.*
>
> **—KENZŌ TANGE**

The Teaching of Kenzō Tange

Other ways to start your firm include teaching. The great Japanese architect Kenzō Tange was a professor at the University of Tokyo in 1946. There he had the opportunity to create the Tange Laboratory, with classrooms in which prestigious architects such as Fumihiko Maki and Arata Isozaki were formed, among others.

Among the important challenges that Tange had in his professional life, one really stands out. Nothing more and nothing less than the commission for the reconstruction of Hiroshima, which had been reduced to ashes by Little Boy, the atomic bomb. Tange built a museum and the Hiroshima Peace Memorial Park, a symbol of pacifism that became a world reference for the modernization of Japan in those times.

What questions did Tange have to ask in order to carry out such assignments? Often, we believe that decisions are made regarding the *what*, but more important than the *what* is the *who*. The most important thing in the development of a company or an office is to select the right people who will accompany you

> THERE ARE NO MAGIC RECIPES ... KEEP MOVING; TIME WILL TELL WHICH RECIPE IS BEST FOR YOU.

in solving challenges. It does not matter if they are temporary, only during the development of that project, or if they are partners in your professional life.

Here I'd like to touch on a topic important to consider: *Solo or with an associate(s)?* The million-dollar question. It is very common for architectural firms to be led initially by two main partners, and generally after a few years, only one of them prevails. In some other cases, especially in the United States, professional development is based on a group of associate architects. There are no magic recipes

… keep moving; time will tell which recipe is best for you. It is the question we must each determine for ourselves.

Returning to Tange, the master was able to be the benchmark of Japanese architecture for most of his professional life, having a firm of multiple associates and architects who teamed up with him. In addition to the monumental Hiroshima project, he also developed multiple buildings for the Tokyo Olympics in 1964, the Japan World Exposition in Osaka in 1970, and more than two hundred other built projects, which attest to his vision and talent.

Tange is proof that being an *architect* and an *entrepreneur* not only works but is the key to any firm being successful.

But what keeps a firm afloat besides recognition? For many years, some have thought that the key is the diversity of projects, having work in different sectors: residential, of course (the sector that I call "the daily bread of every day"), commercial, industrial, corporate, etc. Being a multidisciplinary firm will allow you to work in less-hit industries during recessions. In addition, another of the keys already mentioned is personal relationships; you have to be networking at every possible social event and become "friends" with many prospective clients.

Master Tange's work leads us to understand the Japan of today. His works are found scattered throughout the country, and in them, the closeness to people is reflected as the guiding concept of his designs, creating welcoming urban spaces. He has won numerous awards, being the recipient of the Pritzker Prize, considered the Nobel Prize for architecture, and gold medals from the Royal Institute of British Architects (RIBA), the American Institute of Architects (AIA), and the French Academy of Architecture.

A Book Inspired by an Architect

The Fountainhead, by Ayn Rand, is an extraordinary novel and an essential read for any architect or architecture and book lover. The protagonist is Howard Roark, a brilliant architect who is ready to face everyone in order to defend his individual freedom. Roark, being an uncompromising architect completely devoted to his ideals, is especially a believer that no person should copy another's style, especially in the field of architecture. In addition, the novel tells the story of his violent struggle against the world's standards and conventions of love for a beautiful woman ... his muse, perhaps.

> *Throughout the centuries there were men who took first steps,*
> *down new roads, armed with nothing but their own vision.*
>
> **—AYN RAND**

The novel highlights how relationships are a fundamental part of the development of each one of us during the path of life, whether or not we are architects, whether or not we have a company; it doesn't matter. None of us is an island. What matters is nothing less and nothing more than human interaction and how we handle others or how we influence and connect with others, and this, in turn, forges us with small blows, sometimes subtle and sometimes not so much, during our lives.

> *An idea is salvation by imagination.*
>
> **—FRANK LLOYD WRIGHT**

For many, *The Fountainhead* evoked the personality of another great master: Frank Lloyd Wright, one of the main protagonists of twentieth century architecture. Wright was born in Wisconsin, on a farm, in a poor, religious family. He spent much of his childhood in contact with nature and perhaps this was the key to the conception of his architecture since he is considered a pioneer of organic architecture and the Prairie School movement.

He started studying engineering, but after a short period, he decided to move to Chicago to join the studio of architect J. L. Silsbee, an overly conventional architect for Wright's overflowing creativity. From there, because of that longing for more creativity, he moved on to Adler & Sullivan, with whom he worked for five or so years. Later he ventured to create his own firm, and over the years, history would recognize him as perhaps the best American architect of all time.

His first works were residences that reflected from the beginning his different way of conceptualizing architecture and understanding spaces, with his cross-plan shapes and central spaces that opened to the rest of the inside and provided wonderful lighting. These first expressions were known as Prairie Style Houses, characterized by one- and two-story homes with extensions that created porticos and that worked in harmony with the surrounding nature.

Wright traveled to Japan and Europe, where he was already received as a kind of hero or celebrity. In Japan, he designed the Imperial Hotel, a spectacular building for the time and for the city. In that same year, 1923, a devastating earthquake also took place in Tokyo, which destroyed a good part of the city, but this masterful building resisted and served as a refuge for many people.

One of his Japanese disciples, the architect Arata Endo, wrote him a telegram saying, "what glory to see the Imperial standing in the midst of the ashes of an entire city, glory to you."

An important factor in the life of any architect is travel, the opportunity to learn about other cultures and visit works and spaces created by other architects over the centuries of history. This form of education is without a doubt the best investment we can make.

The career of this giant of American architecture continued until his death at ninety-one years of age. One of Wright's most famous US projects was the Solomon R. Guggenheim Museum in New York, where Wright experimented with space based on a circular design that rises like a whirlwind around a circular central courtyard; it was considered a totally organic and innovative design for the time.

Finding and Learning from Mentors

For all of us, whatever our history may be, decisions are always about the future and our place in it, be it immediate-, medium-, or long-term. So, what is the key to preparing for this? One of the fundamental factors is having the right people with us, that team or that group of mentors who inspire and guide us.

If we analyze different specialties, we can see the elements that are required. Take, for example, tennis as a sport. In addition to the natural ability of a tennis player (how natural their serves and volleys are from an early age, their competitiveness, etc.), there are other factors that can lead to success, like persistence. Getting up every time a set or game is lost, training, consistency, and discipline are all essential for greatness. But the base is motivation, and that comes not only from within but having the right coaches at the appropriate times. I believe such coaches are essential to the work involved in a champion's training. In essence, having the right people at the right time.

I had the opportunity to take a three-year degree at the Massachusetts Institute of Technology (MIT) in 2004, and the first thing I noticed was that we were called the "Class of 2007." I loved the idea that, from the beginning, we already had a goal implicit in the name of our group of cohorts. This is not customary in Latin American countries; students are identified by their *enrollment* year. But I think this minimal change in the way of referring to your "class" achieves a great differential; it sets a goal in time for students to reach for.

And this is what professional life is about, setting goals over and

THE BIGGER THE GOAL, EVEN IF WE ONLY REACH TWO-THIRDS OF IT, PUSHES US TO OUR BEST.

over again, and every time you achieve the first goal, immediately set the second, the third, and so on.

We will always have difficulties or obstacles to achieving our dreams. It is very likely that we will not achieve all of them in their entirety. However, in my particular

point of view, the bigger the goal, even if we only reach two-thirds of it, pushes us to our best. Our achievement will be much higher than that of someone who settles for a very small goal and achieves it in its entirety.

Michelangelo and the Lesson of Relationships

The greatest danger for most of us is not that our goal is too high and we do not reach it, but that it is too low and we do.

—MICHELANGELO

A notable example, not only of talent, but also of knowing how to manage and take advantage of relationships, of having that patron who finances our ideas, is Michelangelo. He found, between Florence and Rome, the Medici family of Florence and the different Roman popes willing to invest in his ideas.

The bigger the work, the bigger the patron who will finance it.

Original, multifaceted, and disruptive, Michelangelo was one of the greatest artists in history. He ventured into different branches of art, all of them with his own particular stamp, and architecture was no exception. Among his most outstanding works are the Florence Laurentian Library, the Piazza Del Campidoglio (Capitol Square) in Rome, and Saint Peter's Basilica in the Vatican, besides his art captured in the dome of the Sistine Chapel.

Michelangelo was actually a genius of three artistic disciplines: painting, sculpture, and, of course, architecture. He marked a before and after in the Renaissance. He was a master of the domes, as seen in the Cathedral of Florence and the Basilica of Saint Peter. Both of his domes were majestic and of a magnificent size for the era, and they are outstanding structural engineering designs in addition to being artistic.

From that point, the master began to use and combine classical and medieval forms, thus marking his architectural style as unique.

Architecture is the learned game, correct and magnificent, of forms assembled in light.

—LE CORBUSIER

Le Corbusier: The Visionary

Another great architect, as well as an entrepreneur, was Le Corbusier. I have mentioned him as an inspiration to many architects throughout this book. Born in 1887, in La Chaux-de-Fonds, Switzerland, he, along with Walter Gropius, undoubtedly marked the international architectural renaissance of the twentieth century.

Le Corbusier was an entrepreneur, cultural instigator, architect, essay writer, idealist, and innovator. He founded the style called purist, a derivation of Picasso and Braque's cubism. He also created a magazine, *L'Espirit Nouveau,* and with his genius he brought the houses of today to life, not only in terms of functionalism but also of the technology of the time, including hot and cold water in each bathroom, food preservation, hygiene, etc.

Le Corbusier was an innovator, who based his architectural contributions on five fundamental points.

1. The use of *pilotis* (structures based on reticular columns)
2. Free design of the ground plan
3. Free design of the façade
4. Horizontal windows
5. Roof gardens and terraces as a bioclimatic strategy

All these were what he considered characteristics of modernism.

The truth is that talking about the master Le Corbusier is talking about *innovation* and *creativity* at its best. As an urban planner, ecologist, and creator of what we now know as apartment buildings, Le Corbusier is a clear example of a thinker and an entrepreneur.

Almost all of us have access to an amazing computer with an extraordinary CPU—our brains! If we were more dedicated to exercising that muscle we call the brain, the world would be very different.

"I think, therefore, I am."

The master, Le Corbusier, had to experience the changes of the Industrial Revolution; with it came new production systems, new construction materials, new ways of projecting and designing, all of which were increasingly closer to engineering. He had to live in times of uniting the concepts of art and technology.

It is our turn to experience the Industrial Revolution 4.0, marked by the convergence of digital, physical, and biological technologies.

CHAPTER FIVE

THE FUTURE IS NOW

TRANSFORMATION

We stand on the brink of a technological revolution that will fundamentally alter the way we live, work, and relate to one another.

—KLAUS SCHWAB, CHAIRMAN OF THE WORLD ECONOMIC FORUM

Previously, humanity experienced three other transformative processes; the first one marked the passage from manual to mechanized production, between 1760 and 1830; the second, around 1865, brought electricity and allowed mass manufacturing. For the third, we had to wait until the middle of the twentieth century, which brought the arrival of electronics and information and telecommunications technology.

Now, the Industrial Revolution 4.0 brings with it a trend toward full automation of manufacturing, but in a completely independent way and via cyber-physical systems, made possible by the internet and cloud computing.

During the past hundred years or so, and due to climate change, among other things, avant-garde architects have been forced to adapt to new challenges, to develop a new architectural style, called sustainable, green, or ecological architecture.

The new normality and the advances of the 4.0 revolution put criteria of energy eco-efficiency at our disposal. We have had to learn to take advantage of natural resources, thus respecting the environment around us. We have smart façades that protect the interior of buildings from solar radiation, with the consequent saving of energy consumption in air conditioning. We also have photovoltaic panels, wind turbines that generate electricity, large green areas that renew the urban fabric, and waste-recycling systems, water-recycling systems, etc.

> *The future of employment will be made of jobs that don't exist in industries that use new technologies, in planetary conditions that no human being has ever experienced.*

—DAVID RITTER, CEO OF GREENPEACE AUSTRALIA PACIFIC

Nanotechnology, robots, artificial intelligence, biotechnology, energy storage systems, drones, 3D printers … you name it. The basic principle is that companies will have the ability to create smart grids that can control themselves, through AI, throughout the value chain. Consequently, the revolution 4.0 could wipe out hundreds of millions of jobs in the world's fifteen most industrialized countries.[2]

THE PACE OF CHANGE IS DIZZYING, AND WE ARE LEFT WITH TWO CHOICES ONLY: ADAPT OR DIE.

---

2   Blue Vision, "What Is Industry 4.0 and How Can It Affect Your Job?," https://bluevision-braskem.com/en/innovation/what-is-industry-4-0-and-how-can-it-affect-your-job/.

Could it be that we architects are ready as a profession? The pace of change is dizzying, and we are left with two choices only: adapt or die.

Here is the importance of attitude versus aptitude. The first is the way in which we face life, circumstances, and problems. The second is whether or not we are fit for that activity or challenge. The second has the advantage that, if we aren't fit, we can learn and develop the skills necessary and thus face that challenge. But your attitude and mindset need to be forward thinking, or all the mentors and education in the world could not help you.

Change or die.

—ALAN DEUTSCHMAN

There is an old Mexican saying: "By force, not even underwear fits."

Attitude is part of your personal makeup. Every action has an equal and opposite reaction. I have always believed that if we maintain a positive attitude above all else, our reactions will go in the same direction and to the same degree of magnitude. As strong as the storm is, that vision of a shining sun will guide our way until we come out ahead, victorious, and ready to continue fighting the next battle.

I don't know why people hire architects,
and then tell them what to do.

—FRANK O. GEHRY

Already established architects surprise us on a daily basis with increasingly avant-garde and environmentally friendly proposals.

One of these geniuses is Frank Gehry, designer of the Guggenheim Museum Bilbao, among other great projects.

Bilbao was a pioneering city in the construction of steel-hull sailing boats. Inspiration comes from everywhere, as architects know. Or rather, we do not know what or when something will inspire us. The Gehry museum gives the feeling of a futuristic sailboat floating on the estuary with all its sails deployed.

And so, architecture changed forever.

Gehry is a precursor of the use, not only of new materials, but also of computer-aided design (CAD). He was an innovator of the change in working models, and he started this when he designed a project for the Olympic Village of Barcelona (1986) using CATIA, a design, manufacturing, and engineering computer program for the aerospace industry. He is an entrepreneur, innovator, and modeler of new ways of working in architecture.

We must always focus on our strengths and not our weaknesses. Think of childhood, when perhaps parents notice that their child is struggling in math; they line up tutors or extra classes. In short, they try to turn that weakness into a strength, or at least level it up. But perhaps, instead, we should discover our strengths and polish them over and over again instead, to turn that rock that we carry inside into the most brilliant of diamonds. This is a paradigm that we must change as a society. Let's educate based on polishing strengths and not creating mediocre people with knowledge of a little of everything, and with their talents forgotten, downplayed, or extinguished.

Gehry won the Pritzker Prize in 1989, the AIA gold medal, the RIBA gold medal, the Presidential Medal of Freedom, and the National Medal of Arts, among other great recognitions. As a good entrepreneur, he also designed jewelry for Tiffany, lamps, and vodka bottles.

Architecture has to be efficiency and truth.

—PEDRO RAMÍREZ VÁZQUEZ

Well, my Mexico is not far behind in terms of great architects, from the Olmecs, Aztecs, Mayans (long before anyone else), to great creators like Pedro Ramírez Vázquez. Ramírez Vázquez was one of the most representative architects of new Mexican architecture, along with the master Luis Barragán (who won the Pritzker Prize in 1980). We currently have excellent representatives of Mexican architecture both nationally and internationally.

The late Ramírez Vázquez would contribute a fundamental part of Mexican culture, the design of the city and its service to the people.

Among other great projects, he carried out the Azteca Stadium and the Basilica of Guadalupe, and also as an excellent entrepreneur, he was entrusted with the complete organization of the 1968 Olympic Games and the 1970 World Cup (which speaks to how versatile he was).

Ramírez Vázquez designed and built much of modern Mexico. He was a great urban planner and visionary as well as a prolific architect and strategist.

I think that success for all of us lies not only in being good at something, but in having the ability to solve the problems that are presented to us, to push forward, to not allow ourselves to be overcome by adversity, and to turn a deaf ear to those voices of *no*, to those little minds that don't understand. Nothing and nobody can prevent us from reaching our goals … only God and ourselves.

We can be whoever we want to be if we just try hard enough. Obstacles are life lessons; the only thing they can achieve is slowing us down in the path to success if we let them.

Just as the phrase for real estate development goes: "Location, location, location." For architecture, it's "relations, relations, relations."

Let's work on our strengths day by day, let's establish a good work team, let's develop a good service or product, and let's work on finances, both personal and those of our company or office.

Today, as work processes change and the world accelerates toward Revolution 4.0, it is important to consider that large offices are no longer necessary, nor is the cost implicit in these.

Let's watch and learn from the YouTubers our children are addicted to, who live in apparent informal employment but earn fortunes. They are a prime example that everything is changing, and if we do not adapt, we will simply become obsolete.

ARCHITECTS NEED TO SEEK THE BEST WAYS TO WORK WITH THE TRANSFORMATIVE POWER OF NEW TECHNOLOGY, MARKETING BRANDING, AND SUSTAINABILITY.

Some YouTubers, bloggers, and Instagrammers are moving trends around the world, and I'm not adding them in here for their content or their exceptional contribution to universal culture but rather for the number of followers that they have. A reflection that times, tastes, and passions are changing abruptly.

But we must recognize that their popularity and weight have reached a point in which many companies today have decided to incorporate them into their work teams to promote their products. Today, the profitability of advertising and promotion of companies resides more noticeably via social networks than via television or print ads, like in the past.

The real challenge, then, is to achieve a good name and online recognition, which can elevate a person to a thought leader on a topic … A multiplier for large brands and companies.

The danger we face is that these people convey "trust," for better or for worse, with the power to change the behavior of consumers or people, particularly that of young and impressionable minds.

We're living in times of rapid change. As architects, we need to seek the best ways to work with the transformative power of new technology, marketing, and branding and need to keep in mind sustainability.

There has never been a time of greater
promise, or greater danger.

—KLAUS SCHWAB

CHAPTER SIX

COLLABORATION, CREATION, AND INNOVATION

THE ELEMENTS OF SUCCESS

*In the 21st century, architecture will continue as in the times
of the pyramids, being a fundamental art to improve people's
lives, to define the identity of the time in which we live.*

—SANTIAGO CALATRAVA

The Valencian, Santiago Calatrava, has something that many architects dream of. And I'm not just referring to his talent in design but
the fact that he managed to pursue two careers that, mixed with
talent, make an extraordinary pair: architecture and civil engineering. Calatrava is an innovator in the design of bridges and structures,

such as the Alamillo Bridge in Seville and the Kuwait Pavilion at the Seville Expo '92.

In 2005, works such as the expansion of the Milwaukee Art Museum, the James Joyce Bridge in Dublin, the Sóndica Airport in Bilbao, and the Auditorium of Santa Cruz de Tenerife, earned him the American Institute of Architects gold medal, placing him at the height of greats like Frank Lloyd Wright, Louis Sullivan, Le Corbusier, and Louis Kahn.

One is born with genius, or so we believe. Talent can be exercised for it to become a strength. A few years ago, I read a study involving children with musical "genius"—in this case on the piano—children who, from the age of three or four, already demonstrated that innate talent. At the same time, children with a liking for the piano, but without the genius of the previous ones, were studied. The result, after years of lessons, is that genius and talent/practice evened out.

What the study shows is that we can develop our skills to such an extent that if we invest enough time in them, we can turn them into strengths, those skills can reach almost perfection if we apply ourselves.

And what about our weaknesses? We certainly recognize them because they normally involve what we least like doing. In my particular case as an architect, I believe that my blind spot and my greatest weakness is and always has been in financial management, and I never knew how important it was to find my counterpart. An excellent way to turn a weakness into a strength is to find a partner who fills up that space in which we are deficient. And I do not necessarily mean another architect. In my case, for example, I would be better complemented by a business administrator or an accountant. And why a partner and not an employee? Precisely because of the degree of commitment that is required, it has to be someone who gives themself to the project as much as we do, someone who really shares the feeling of responsibility and reacts in their own area as we do in ours. Essentially, the Robin to our Batman, the Watson to our Sherlock Holmes, the Spock to our Captain Kirk, or the Chewbacca to our Han Solo.

There is something in common in the stories of successful cofounders; each member of the pair knows perfectly what they are good at and lets the other work in the areas they know they are limited in. Instead of building a divided company, they build a company in which they complement each other, an addition of the genius or talent of both.

We need an accomplice in this adventure called entrepreneurship and transformation, such as Steve Jobs and Steve Wozniak from Apple or Mark Zuckerberg and Eduardo Saverin from Meta, who started together, no matter if they later separated.

Many others remain or remained together for many years, such as Larry Page and Sergey Brin from Google (1996), Bill Hewlett and Dave Packard from HP (1938), William Procter and James Gambler from Procter & Gambler (1837), Daniel Ek and Martin Lorentzon from Spotify (2006), or Walt and Roy Disney from the Walt Disney Company (1923).

The formula is variable. In many cases, it starts with friends from school, or perhaps family; others at first did not get along well, or maybe they were competitors, but they shared a common passion that led them to identify themselves to such a degree that they decided, at some point in their lives, to work toward a common project.

In 2014, I was invited to collaborate as a partner representative of Mexico in an extraordinary international architecture firm, RMJM, its main office being in Edinburgh, Scotland. Founded by Robert Matthew and Johnson Marshall in 1956, RMJM is to this day one of the largest architecture and design networks in the world. In 1967, they had 350 associates and employees, an amount that was surprising for the year, and currently they have offices in nearly thirty countries on five continents. The unique opportunity to collaborate and see the development of such large and important projects opens your eyes to the possibilities, lets you see that in union there is strength, that what unites us is greater than what separates us, and that the world really has no borders.

Our firm, CEARC, was born in Monterrey in 1992, right when I graduated from the Instituto Tecnologico y de Estudios Superiores de Monterrey (ITESM). Via the entrepreneurial program, we partici-pated in and obtained one of the first two TEC support investments for student companies through SINCA PROITESM in 1994. This opened up the possibility of growing in the Monterrey market and consolidating our company. In 1996, I bought the shares of TEC, and I remained a sole partner. Today, over thirty years later,

> SOMETIMES BECAUSE OF BUDGET OR SIZE, WE MUST DEVELOP ARCHITECTURE TO OBTAIN THE GREATEST ECONOMIC UTILITY FOR THE CLIENT THROUGH EFFICIENT DESIGN.

we continue tirelessly fighting for our convictions and our ideals, aiming to achieve the goal of transcendence through the poetry that we call architecture.

We had many ups and downs during this time, but always the satisfaction of delivering and leaving a mark with our projects. We have designed and built from large-scale buildings of twelve thousand square meters, on down to small projects. This is the real challenge; sometimes because of the budget or the size of the lot and regulations, we must try to develop not only to fulfill the need of architecture but also to meet the need to obtain the greatest economic utility for the client through an efficient design, not only in facilities but also in not wasting square meters. To achieve this, we have focused on analyzing the target market and objective of the client, polishing our design offer to carefully and thoughtfully analyze all the variables.

We can't conceive the design without all the elements, from finance to customer needs, from space and form to construction balance and technical efficiency.

Each and every one of us attacks the design process in different ways. Whatever our process, we have an obligation to the project, its environment, and above all, the user and surrounding users; there must always be a balance of all parts.

Architecture is responsibility.

Our studio has recently been working on real estate development projects for the reconstruction or reconditioning of spaces, transforming them not only with new architecture but also with a sustainable business plan to create business models based on the reuse of real estate spaces.

We recently transformed vacant commercial spaces into an office model for a full-service physicians' private practice with a return on investment in less than three years and margins of 32 percent per year. Our business models, like the one we are studying in a suburb near Monterrey, also seek to develop areas devoid of services, areas that lead their inhabitants to travel long hours to find work or, as in this case, a good technical education, but under a sustainable model that will have a technical university, a commercial area with restaurants, a cultural area, and also a BMX track to have a mix of services and businesses that bring work to this area and attract users from other areas to entertain themselves with exercise or cultural activities.

As architects, we still have a long way to go; everything depends on fine-tuning our vision and our offered services.

Since the pandemic, many forms of work have changed. So, too, the real estate market has changed, as I have previously stated. Office buildings, for sure, are changing in their purpose, so there is a big opportunity for architects to create new uses for those large spaces, not only as a request from clients but through the creation of new real estate business models.

Mixed-use developments will grow and evolve, and new forms of leisure and social coexistence will appear as a consequence of this.

In our model, a tech base university will be an anchor that will make the model we are developing economically sustainable and will provide many students who, in turn, together with their families and external visitors, will give life and utilize the small businesses around the plaza. For the community, having a center of education nearby where they can send their children for higher learning without incurring large transportation or residence costs will conserve time and economic resources. A win-win situation for sure.

The world is made up of a sum of efforts, and all efforts count.

Stephen Hawking and Albert Einstein are two brilliant minds who examined time and its role in our universe. It is up to us to treasure each moment and make the most of our existence. Our lives are formed step by step; many times we will not know why we took that direction, but we discover that it was the right one, not because of the result, but because of the learning. The important thing is to really learn and take advantage of every moment.

When things go wrong, just swing. Countless companies started out as one thing but ended up successful in another. More than two hundred years ago, Eli Whitney transformed his business from a cotton gin factory into an arms factory. Whitney was an entrepreneur and visionary, and he bet everything on that dream, offering to manufacture ten thousand muskets in record time for the American government. At that time, the manufacture of weapons was an art, the manufacture of assembly parts was manual, and the war against France was approaching. His formula? *Time.*

Cornelius Vanderbilt was a billionaire pioneer who made his fortune by transporting goods by ship. As a good visionary, he managed to identify that his business would be nothing against the future railroad, so he sold his merchant fleet and built tracks to connect the east and the west by land, much faster than by ship. He pivoted, he swayed, following his vision as an entrepreneur and businessman.

> *We architects are a different species, one accustomed to constantly pivoting to see beyond and to transform not only our environment but ourselves, so if today you are stuck ... go further and transform yourself. After two of the most difficult and divisive years in living memory, architects have a unique opportunity to show the world what we do best: Put forward ambitious and creative ideas that help us imagine a more equitable and optimistic future in common.*

—LESLEY LOKKO

Innovation, Reengineering, Transformation

Whatever our profession, we must rediscover ourselves at every moment, especially today in this changing world so given to throw away the old. As my daughters tell me, "That song is old—it came out a month ago." This is the dizzying speed of today's life. Anything that cannot transcend its own useful life becomes obsolete in an instant.

Fortunately, through architecture, our projects that see the light are built to be seen by thousands and for many years ... for better or for worse.

Here lies the great responsibility of the architect, that of contributing to improving our society, designing spaces that invite reflection, peace, and transformation; spaces that respect the environment and the location in which they will be built.

When we were immersed in quarantine (fourth-wave version) from COVID-19, I saw how life rapidly transformed and how we adapted to it, especially through my daughters: Vanessa, my architecture student, made electronic models and took classes online; Elsa watched her friends from high school through a screen; Camila, the youngest of my three, recorded videos for her sports class and uploaded them over the network and to the cloud, to a server where coaches would see her progress. It seems crazy, or just another chapter of the cartoons *The Jetsons* or *Futurama*.

THE GREAT RESPONSIBILITY OF THE ARCHITECT IS TO CONTRIBUTE TO SOCIETY AND DESIGN SPACES THAT INVITE REFLECTION, PEACE, AND TRANSFORMATION.

Those devices that unite the distant ones and separate the close ones, those from which we would like to disconnect our children from time to time so that, just as we did when we were little, they can play out in the streets again, dirty their clothes with mud, climb trees, eat green mangos with salt, scrape their knees, cry, get lost for hours without knowing for sure where they are, but knowing that they are fine.

The important thing about these technologies is to know how to take advantage of them and get the best out of them without wasting that nonrenewable good that is called *time*. As the genius Albert Einstein (supposedly) said, "When a man sits with a pretty girl for an hour, it seems like a minute. But let him sit on a hot stove for a minute, and it will seem like more than an hour ... that's relativity."

Time is a "physical" tool with which we measure the duration or separation of events. I invite you to pause briefly and take a minute—timed—to be still and quiet in silence, and you will see how tremendously spacious that minute can be. Just as if we were to watch the result of a Formula 1 race and establish the position of the champion in comparison to the one who finished in tenth place … a minute can be eternal. But if it were to be what we have left to finish an exam, on the contrary, it passes very quickly.

Mentioning the paradox of the twins suffices: One twin stays on Earth, while the other goes into space at a high speed to Polaris, turns around, and returns home. When he arrives, he has only aged six months, while his brother is already an old man. It is not a biological phenomenon but of a property of time, which is delayed when we move very fast.

We can learn how to manage time in our favor, it's as easy as using a daily schedule and keeping track of goals and deadlines.

Time is the eternal challenge for everything we do. It's amazing sometimes how easily it slips through our hands. We waste this non-renewable good on so many superfluous things like our cell phones. When will we learn?

What we must know is collaboration, innovation, and creation are the foundations of success—and with limited time, that precious commodity, the time to be inspired … is *now!*

Your time is limited. Don't waste it living someone else's dream.

—STEVE JOBS

CHAPTER SEVEN

HEROINES OF ARCHITECTURE

WOMEN VISIONARIES

Ignore the glass ceiling and do your work.

—AVA DUVERNAY

Today is the time for women, who, little by little and by their own effort and constant struggle, are occupying the most important positions in each area they enter. In these times of revolution, I see more and more the presence of a new superhero, a stronger, more determined, more independent one, the empowered woman—women with the strength to achieve everything they set out to do. Forces of nature.

"Yes, I'm a feminist, because I see all women as smart, gifted, and tough," commented Zaha Hadid in an interview in Russia in 2012.

Historically, the world of architecture was for men only, but the effort of thousands of women is already tipping the scales. As I recall, when I started studying this profession in 1987 in Guatemala, we were 65 percent males as a percentage. Today, that number has already turned around to about 52 percent women.

Today I want to pay tribute to each and every one of them, not only to the architects, but also to all my colleagues, professionals, mothers, wives, and daughters.

> *I think what you are not receiving makes you more*
> *persevering. I could have thrown in the towel, but I didn't*
> *because I knew there was a lot to unearth, to discover.*
> *Interpret each "no" as a "keep going," as a challenge.*
>
> **—ZAHA HADID**

The woman who changed everything was Zaha Hadid. She was a deconstructivist architect, born in Iraq, who studied architecture in London and was fortunate enough to have great masters, such as the Dutchman Rem Koolhass (Pritzker 2000), who undoubtedly influenced her architectural conception. Upon graduation, she worked at the Office for Metropolitan Architecture (OMA) in Rotterdam, the renowned studio of Koolhass and Zenghelis. There she met Peter Rice, the engineer who would make possible her incredible structures, her extraordinary projects: Her robin.

After that, Hadid decided to create her own office, Zaha Hadid Architects, based in London, and in 1980, after exhibiting at the MOMA in NY in the exhibition "Deconstructivism in Architecture," her fame shot up, and she carried out extraordinary projects such as the Heydar Aliyev Cultural Centre in Baku, the Guangzhou Opera House in China, and the London Aquatics Centre. In short, each one more revealing and challenging to the canons of architecture and art.

Hadid became the first woman to receive the Architecture Pritzker in 2004, in addition to the Mies van der Rohe Prize and the Stirling Prize. She was appointed Commander of the Order of the British Empire (CBE), and she was also the first woman to receive the RIBA gold medal.

She dedicated much of her life to teaching at the University of Chicago, Columbia, and Yale; in addition, at Harvard University she held the Kenzō Tange chair at the Graduate School of Design. As an entrepreneur, she designed furniture and consumer products like the Z.Car, a futuristic three-wheeler powered by hydrogen. She designed shoes for Lacoste and even had her own clothing brand, which she wore almost daily.

In our profession, another heroine was Gae Aulenti, an Italian architect. She had the privilege of doing the project to remodel the Orsay station in Paris, as well as the restoration of the Palazzo Grassi, transforming it into a museum. Throughout almost sixty years of professional life, she had the opportunity to work in industrial design, interior design, and even theatrical scenery.

Our colleague, Lina Bo Bardi, Brazil's best kept secret, developed together with the masters Lucio Costa and Oscar Niemeyer a powerful architecture with modern roots very attached to the best Brazilian traditions. Like her heroine peers in the chapter, she was creative and visionary.

Kasuyo Sejima, a disciple of Toyo Ito, obtained the Pritzker with her colleague Ryue Nishizawa in 2010. She uses diagrammatic architecture, a style that exploits transposition and instrumentalization. One of her most relevant works is the New Museum of Contemporary Art in New York.

Spain's Carme Pigem, born in Girona, obtained the Pritzker in 2017 along with her partners Rafael Aranda and Ramón Vilalta.

Among her most important works lies the natural park of the volcanic area of La Garrotxa (La Garrocha), where much of the work is dominated by the interrelation with the landscape of Olot, where she attended university.

Recently the 2020 Pritzker was awarded to Yvonne Farrell and Shelley McNamara, both Irish and friends from University College Dublin. Their style of architecture starts from a humanistic approach, respecting time, heritage, tradition, and people.

TODAY WOMEN HAVE MORE OPPORTUNITIES TO COMPETE AND DOMINATE IN ALL THE SCENARIOS IN WHICH THEY APPEAR.

Although we still have much work to do, today women have more opportunities to compete and dominate in all the scenarios in which they appear. This gives me much encouragement as a father since my daughters, like many other women, will be able to develop in a more just and balanced world.

I am a deep admirer of women, of their strength and courage, of how, despite living in a world manipulated by men, they have known how to excel and demonstrate their talent every day. I have been blessed with smart and talented daughters and an amazing wife. I was raised by a wonderful mother. I have had the opportunity to work with many women in my life, collaborators and architects, and I have learned something from each one of them. I appreciate their contribution to my professional career and my vision of the increasingly important influence of women in all sectors and movements that are changing our world for better.

We form a complement. Every day more women lead and collaborate with their male counterparts, not only in architecture but also in every discipline.

Women and men are complementary of each other in every single activity from the most insignificant to the more important. We form the most perfectly imperfect team that can exist. We not only shape our ventures but also the future of humanity.

So, stop the inequality. We have to keep moving forward. If women, who account for half the world's working-age population, do not achieve their full economic potential, our common development will suffer. Most families now depend on the economic empowerment and productivity of women.

IF WOMEN, WHO ACCOUNT FOR HALF THE WORLD'S WORKING-AGE POPULATION, DO NOT ACHIEVE THEIR FULL ECONOMIC POTENTIAL, OUR COMMON DEVELOPMENT WILL SUFFER.

This last push to improve gender equality has to come from the roots, from the education of our children from kindergarten, and from the example that adults set in our daily behavior.

CHAPTER EIGHT

MOTIVATION, LEADERSHIP, AND THE FUTURE

WHERE DO WE GO FROM HERE?

I lost motivation, so I retired.

—BJORN BORG

With eleven Grand Slam titles in tennis, Bjorn Borg was just twenty-six years of age when he decided to retire, and even today he is considered one of the five greats of tennis worldwide. Young Borg lost the angel of motivation, the one who is indispensable for everyone in any activity, and the most unexpected reaction was that of his archrival on the court, the great John McEnroe.

The world of sports has left us rivalries that mark a before and an after; there have been such incredible ones, and there will continue

63

to be new ones forever. One of those extraordinary rivalries would change tennis forever; it was born in the 1980 Wimbledon final, and it is still considered today perhaps the best tennis match in history.

McEnroe learned of Borg's retirement after winning the US Open, just a few minutes after the match. Coming out of the locker room, a journalist broke the news to him, and after a minute of silence, McEnroe broke it, saying, "Now who am I going to beat?" For him, Borg was his motivation.

We never really know where we are going to get our motivation from, but there it is, waiting for us to hold onto it and let it bring out the best in us, to achieve that goal that is often just ours. We all have deeply personal goals, simply our final of 1980.

Architecture makes us fight battles, with pencil and paper in the beginning, with the mouse later. And for each of those battles, we cling to a goal that motivates us; perhaps it is to design the highest project, the most original, the largest, or sometimes, it's the challenge of a very small area, of a project with budget limitations, or, as Frank Lloyd Wright said when asked what his best project was, he simply replied, "the next one."

The Tallest

The tallest … for now. When we talk about challenges, goals, and of course, motivations, what better example than the project's allocation for the world's tallest tower? I am referring to the Burj Khalifa (BK) tower, from the Skidmore, Owings & Merrill firm, the design led by architect Adrian Smith. We are talking about an 828-meter tower designed in a "Y" shape inspired by the *Hymenocallis* flower (or Spider Lily), and elements of Islamic architecture.

Before the BK, the tallest tower was the Taipei 101 (2004/ninth tallest today) at 508 meters high. What challenges do we face when trying to design a tower 300 meters higher and on sand, for example? Ugh, it's crazy. But only madmen and madwomen with vision and an excellent multidisciplinary team can accomplish that feat.

Then we are reminded again, not the *what*, but rather the *who*. Professionally, for many types of goals (and not only in architecture), we have to have a capable team of professionals who support us and encourage us to become effective leaders.

LEADERSHIP + TEAM = SUCCESS

Only in this way can we face challenges professionally. Many times, these teams are temporary and/or external. Sometimes they are mentors or coaches, and other times they are an integral and permanent part of our companies. But yes, everyone counts, from those who have the smallest function to those who have the largest. We already know the saying, "The rope always breaks from the weakest point." So, we should not underestimate anyone on the team, and as leaders, we must be the example.

When I took the Birthing of Giants (BOG) diploma from MIT in conjunction with Entrepreneurs Organization (EO), excellently led by Verne Harnish, the growth guru, they made us see that any company that seeks to exceed and prevail needs to focus on four fundamental areas:

1. **Who:** Build a team of effective people.
2. **Strategy:** This must be very well defined, and everyone must be aligned to it.

THE **49%** ARCHITECT, **51%** ENTREPRENEUR

3. **Execution:** Effectiveness when executing, doing more with less.
4. **Cash:** "Cash is king;" reduce the time in which the cash flow returns (CCC/Cash Conversion Cycle).

So being a leader, having an excellent well-motivated team, having a well-defined and shared strategy with our staff, executing professionally, and of course, taking care of the flows and the economic balance are fundamental factors for any company.

> *Getting together is the beginning. Keeping together*
> *is progress. Working together is success.*
>
> **—HENRY FORD**

Father of mass production, Henry Ford revolutionized transportation and industry in the United States. He was a prolific inventor who obtained 161 patents, and after several failures, managed to succeed, founding the Ford Motor Company. Part of his success was because he offered his workers a higher salary; they earned double what they were used to, and thus he achieved the loyalty of his work team … his *who*.

He managed to turn his passion for cars into a company, where he developed his ability to impose his strategy and innovate by making cars accessible to the middle class of the time.

> *To innovate is to find new or improved uses*
> *of resources that we already have.*
>
> **—PETER DRUCKER**

Speaking of innovation, imagine that the year is 1886, and you are challenged to design and build a symbol for your city, a symbol that in 1889 will be celebrated at the Universal Exposition … yes, we are in Paris.

A man made the decision to create the tallest tower in the world, something never done before, in addition to using an innovative material for it, such as iron, and all this under a unique design. I'm talking about Gustav Eiffel, whom we met earlier in the book, and his magnanimous tower, which bears his last name.

It was a tremendous challenge, and more so for the time, not only in design but also in execution, and especially with the prede- termined deadline that simply had to be met. Entrepreneurs, in this case engineers, had to hire, train, and lead a team of extraordinary people to bring this important work to life. Furthermore, they had to have had the correct strategy, reengineer it several times, and execute it almost perfectly and on budget.

It should be noted that Eiffel was the entrepreneur, Maurice Koechlin and Emile Nouguier were the engineers, and Stephen Sauvestre, the architect. These people were selected from 107 par- ticipating teams in a design contest. And although the project was highly criticized during and after its construction, today it is, without a doubt, the symbol of France and an extraordinary contributor to its economy.

There is an attraction and charm inherent in the
colossal that is not subject to ordinary theories of art.
The tower will be the tallest edifice ever raised by man.
Will it, therefore, be imposing in its own way?

—GUSTAV EIFFEL

Talent and success do not always go hand in hand. If you don't believe it, you'll have to ask the Dutch painter Vincent Van Gogh, or the writer Edgar Allan Poe, or the scientist of alternating electricity, Nikola Tesla. In short, there are many who achieved fame until after death, or sacrificed wealth in life, or could not sell a single painting.

We do not always make the right decisions that lead us to maximize our talents. Other times we do not take advantage when we are at the top, or we simply allow ourselves to be overwhelmed by external situations that we cannot control, and all this leads us to not properly take advantage of our opportunities and talents.

Many times, we need a break in our lives, a time just for us, to think without the distraction of current technology, a time to reflect and do our own reengineering. Two years ago, misfortune gave us that opportunity. Quarantine was a "pause" for many, and I hope that we have all taken advantage of this forced break.

The worst moments define us, and our actions determine the result. Everything is cause and effect.

The history of the Lakhta Center, an 87-story, 462-meter-high skyscraper in Russia, is proof of the effort a project requires to be carried out. The tower was designed by Tony Kettle, RMJM architect, after winning a design competition in 2006, despite competing against

TALENT CAN BE BORN, BUT SUCCESS MUST BE EARNED.

architects who had won prestigious office projects such as Daniel Libeskind and Rem Koolhaas. From the start, the project raised a lot of controversy, as the Eiffel Tower did at the time. Due to the controversies (some of it having to do with its location and the marshy land it was to be built on), the three architects of the jury— Norman Foster, Rafael Viñoly, and Kisho Kurokawa— resigned. The decision was then left to the rest of the jury and a public poll. The commotion was so much that even the chess player Garry Kasparov marched through the streets of Saint Petersburg in protest against the project.

In the end, the project was carried out and completed in 2019, making it the tallest building in Europe … just like the Eiffel Tower at the time.

We'll see what time says. In my particular point of view, the Lakhta Tower is an extraordinary example of avant-garde architecture and will undoubtedly be a new icon for Saint Petersburg.

RMJM is led by my good friend Peter Morrison, a bold entrepreneur with a vision of what the future of architectural firms should be. He is revolutionizing the way architectural offices are transformed, via studies of semi-independent associates worldwide.

Human ingenuity is always behind innovative architecture, sometimes by chance or whim of nature, and sometimes thanks to technology or cutting-edge structural systems. The Leaning Tower of Pisa, the bell tower of the cathedral of the same name located in Italian Tuscany, owes its inclination of approximately four degrees to a whim of weight against the type of soil. Today, it is a World Heritage Site and, thanks to the work done to stabilize it, we will be able to enjoy this wonder for many more years.

Still today, the record for the world's most leaning tower is held by another RMJM project. I'm referring to the leaning tower of Abu Dhabi—The Capital Gate. The 35-level 169-meter-high building, that opened in 2010, has an inclination of eighteen degrees. The structure rests on a base of 490 piles at a depth of thirty meters, providing stability against wind, gravitational traction, and seismic pressures that arise due to the inclination of the building.

Once again, we see that a good *team,* with an excellent *strategy,* and magnificent *execution,* as well as a very good client—cash is king—achieves extraordinary projects.

Beauty perishes in life but is immortal in art.

—LEONARDO DA VINCI

Currently the tower that holds the second place in the world in terms of height is the Shanghai Tower of 632 meters by the architectural firm Gensler. Considered one of the "greenest" buildings on Earth, this formidable project not only recycles rainwater, but its glass façade also transforms wind into clean energy.

One-third of the entirety of this building is dedicated to green spaces. Upon entering it, you can see gardens and walls covered with vegetation. Every fourteen levels you reach a public square and, last but not least, it has three green atriums of fourteen floors each.

This formidable building has a second glass skin, which works by letting the outside air enter, refreshing the interior space and saving energy in air conditioning consumption.

Responsible Sustainability

Sustainability is not a trend. It has arrived and taken hold and is here to stay, and if as an architect you are not aware of and committed to it—go look for another profession.

Sustainability and social contribution are also reflected in the new Toronto Public Library building. In addition to having a strong social function within its community, including information on obtaining citizenship for new immigrants to Canada, it has a community garden that serves to grow certain foods that are watered with the water collected from the rains. It also uses clean energy from photovoltaic panels and greatly encourages alternative mobility.

Many of these new sustainable projects have LEED (Leadership in Energy & Environmental Design) certification, a project certification and environmental design system that applies to single-family homes as well as buildings, neighborhoods, and eventually cities.

To qualify for this certificate, buildings must be designed and built under eco-efficiency standards and must meet sustainability requirements.

The certification evaluates six criteria.

1. Site sustainability
2. Water efficiency and use
3. Materials and natural resources used
4. Energy efficiency, consumption, and greenhouse gas emissions
5. Quality of the interior environment and innovation in the design process
6. Carbon footprint

The benefits of LEED construction are, among others, a lower cost of operation, reduction of waste, optimization of energy and water, and healthier environments both indoors and outdoors by reducing the emission of harmful gases into the atmosphere.

It seems that we are returning to the healthy customs of our ancestors. In pre-Columbian Mexico, the Mexicas developed an artificial cultivation system in which water was the main natural resource. They were built in order to grow plants, greens, and vegetables for self-consumption and the local market, at the same time allowing fish to develop under them, promoting fishing. This innovative productivity system allowed the conservation of lake areas, which in turn, being complex ecosystems full of life, had beneficial effects on climate and air quality.

Under the name of Chinampas, these ecosystems were declared a World Heritage Site by UNESCO in 1987.

The future of sustainability and the Industrial Revolution 4.0 are closely linked.

Imagine your house scheduling a date for maintenance on its own, and then, on that date, it does all the work to stay like new. Or imagine hundreds of homes for the homeless, designed by artificial intelligence and built with 3D printers.

Today, architects have many more tools to help us design not only sustainably, but also in the near future we will have elements or materials that self-repair, that grow according to the user's needs, or spaces that are transformed with the arrival of a new tenant. Three-dimensional printing can lead us to have 0 percent waste, all while achieving perfect thermal and acoustic insulation.

Can you imagine using algae to light up a room and, at the same time, take care of the environment? There are multiple developers working on these systems. One of them is a young Mexican green-tech entrepreneur, Adán Ramirez Sanchez. His bio-panel, which is characterized by its particular green triangular shape, can be placed almost anywhere, serving as a window, ceiling, skylight, or wall. Thanks to this, Adam was recognized as one of the thirty-five innovators under thirty-five in 2019 by the *MIT Technology Review.*

But what about our cities? How are they going to transform? Today, there is a community or small city that can give us an idea of where we are going on this issue: Masdar City located in Abu Dhabi, within the United Arab Emirates.

Masdar City is an effort by leading world institutions such as MIT, Siemens, the Worldwide Fund for Nature, and the United Arab Emirates, among others. This extraordinary project has a perimeter wall, which will help contain the region's sandstorms without hindering the ventilation provided by the air currents. It has a wind tower that channels all the air toward the ground, managing to refresh its pedestrian alleys. The entire city derives its energy from solar panels, operates water desalination, dehumidification, and refrigeration systems. All the water comes from the sea and from gray and black water treatment.

It is designed so that no one has a car, and transport through the city depends on three systems.

1. The first is a personal-type transport (PRT), which consists of an individual cabin that will cover the entire city in seven minutes. It will have eighty-five stations and work 24-7.
2. The second, the light rail-type transport (LRT), is an electric train that will connect directly with the outside world and the Abu Dhabi airport.
3. The third will be the fully automated fast-freight transport (FRT).

Although part of the city is already operating, this gigantic multidisciplinary effort is expected to be ready sometime before 2025.

CHAPTER NINE

ENTREPRENEURS OF ARCHITECTURE II

LEARNING FROM MORE OF THE WORLD'S MASTERS

Every new situation requires a new architecture.

—JEAN NOUVEL

We have still more architects to learn from, to be inspired by. I present here some more innovators, shaking things up in the architecture world.

Jean Nouvel

One of the most innovative and controversial architects of recent times had a childhood marked by the deficiencies and restrictions typical of the postwar period. In 1976, Jean Nouvel founded French Architects, a progressive movement that advocated for the active participation of architects in decision-making areas, such as urban policy and heritage management. The following year, he founded the Architecture Union. A creative and activist, Nouvel won the Pritzker in 2008. In 1982, he jumped into the international arena by winning the design competition for the Arab World Institute, a project designed so that it could be perceived from the outside in different ways from any angle.

In 2001, he was awarded the project for the Agbar Tower in Barcelona, a spectacular cylindrical building crowned by a dome and covered with sixteen thousand sheets of translucent glass that change color according to the intensity and variations of sunlight.

In recent times, he has been known as the creator of the Louvre Abu Dhabi. He sees it as a "welcoming world that serenely combines light and shadow, reflection and calm." The project is based on an important symbol of Arab architecture: the dome. In this case, one formed by a double dome 180 meters in diameter, offering a perfectly radial horizontal geometry. A randomly perforated woven material providing shade with bursts of sunlight.

Nouvel has known how to navigate any waters that he found himself in. Perhaps he did not expect to reach so many ports, but I know he never stopped rowing every time it was required.

The crisis forces you to do more with less. Some of the
best projects arise from the greatest difficulties.

—NORMAN FOSTER

Norman Foster

Norman Foster, awarded multiple times and knighted by Queen Elizabeth in 1990, is arguably one of the most gifted minds in architecture. Among his most acclaimed projects are the building for the Shanghai Banking Corporation in Hong Kong, the 30 Saint Mary

Axe tower in London (which I find particularly extraordinary), the renovation of the Reichstag building in Berlin, the megaproject of the international airport of Hong Kong and the Commerzbank Tower in Frankfurt.

In addition to having a renowned law firm, he created the Norman Foster Foundation, which encourages interdisciplinary thinking and research to support new generations of architects, designers, and urban planners in anticipating the future.

The foundation believes in the importance of connecting architecture, design, technology, and the arts to better serve society. What better legacy can a man leave to society than just his work? In this case, Foster goes further and through this extraordinary initiative, this wonderful foundation, he leaves us his vision turned into education for the future.

One of the foundation's missions has been to raise awareness of the plight of slum dwellers across the globe, who currently number one billion people. If nothing is done, this could mean one of every three inhabitants of the planet in 2050. His studio is also currently working on developing and theorizing about the first human constructions on the moon and on Mars.

Norman Foster is a genius turned architect. He is the perfect example of an architect entrepreneur, a visionary, a person who not only thinks, but also realizes and transforms. Of course, this cannot be achieved without suffering or without fighting. Like everyone, Foster certainly had to fight the *no* at every step of the way in his life.

So let us reflect on what we want for ourselves. What will our legacy be? It does not matter the size of it, but rather the quality of the legacy that we leave, it can be only to our

> WHAT WILL OUR LEGACY BE? ITS SIZE DOES NOT MATTER, BUT RATHER THE QUALITY OF OUR LEGACY.

family, which would be magnificent, or it can be to our community, city, country, or the whole world, which would be extraordinary.

Light is used as a metaphor of the Good in all its perfection, in the meaning attributed by philosophers, poets, painters, musicians, politicians and popes. In architecture as in any other creative expression, light has always been a source of ecstasy and of inspiration.

—RICHARD MEIER

Richard Meier

This valuable representative of North American architecture, Richard Meier (Pritzker 1984) began his professional career at nothing more and nothing less than the renowned firm Skidmore, Owings, & Merrill (SOM) and later with Marcel Breuer, one of the main masters of the modern movement. In 1972, he was identified as one of "the five" in New York, an architectural group consisting of Peter Eisenman, Michael Graves, Charles Gwathmey, and John Hejduk.

Among his most recognized works is the High Museum of Art in Atlanta; the Atheneum in New Harmony, Indiana; the Getty Center in Los Angeles; and the Jubilee Church in Rome.

From the beginning Meier has followed a determined permanent style and line in his projects. He has left his imprint on both temporary and permanent trends, and one of his idols who has notoriously influenced his work was Le Corbusier.

The Traits of Entrepreneur Architects

In short, the paths that led to the success of all these extraordinary architects have been different, but they still have aspects in common, in addition to their artistic genius.

First, each and every one of them is an entrepreneur. They are people who have not been beaten, regardless of the size of the challenge. They focused their gaze on one point and never turned away. They have faith in themselves; if you don't believe in yourself, nobody will.

Second, they managed to establish a team of collaborators with whom they shared a common vision and have managed to lead that team toward that point, that goal.

Third, they are "simple" people, and I mean they see a way out in everything; they are not complicated. They know that they are the best in the world at something, and they focus on this great advantage.

Fourth, they have a culture of discipline, which allows progress without internal bureaucracy. When they master this internal culture, they achieve an incredible performance in their companies.

Fifth, they have the most advanced technological tools, and their teams master them, use them, and are not used by them.

And if those tools don't exist, they create them. Let's remember the beginning of CAD, which went from something used in another industry to being adopted by architects, precisely thanks to the curiosity of those architects who adopted it and adapted it to our industry.

We all have qualities that can be developed individually or as a complement to the quality of another. It is important that we seek, without wasting time, what we are good at, and how we can complement others. This we must do in order to, together or individually, improve our environment.

Limitless

When the new roof of the world is completed at the beginning of this decade, the Jeddah Tower will be almost a kilometer high, in this competition that will lead us one day to achieve Frank Lloyd Wright's dream of the "one-mile-high building."

In such a case, when it is finished, this work will have impressive figures. Its observatory terrace will be 644 meters above the ground. We should note that the observatory of the Empire State Building is only 373 meters high and that the observatory on the 148th floor of the Burj Khalifa is 555 meters above the ground.

This wonder of architecture and engineering was designed by Adrian Smith and Gordon Gill. Smith is also honored to have designed what is so far the tallest tower in the world, the Burj Khalifa, while working for SOM.

The Jeddah Tower design is inspired by the folded leaves of desert vegetation. If this sounds familiar, it may be because it's similar to the inspiration behind the Burj Khalifa. It will also feature the most advanced technology to date.

In this battle to reach the skies, Dubai seems to be reluctant to lose the lead. In a project called Dubai Creek, an even higher structure is being imagined. It is a Santiago Calatrava project whose final size remains a mystery.

When we made the Burj Khalifa, the client's desire was to
make the tallest building, and that led to giving identity
to the development of the houses that surround it, so the
Downtown Dubai gave people an element of identity,
and the client, all the success in terms of development,
and also generated income for the city from tourism.

—ADRIAN SMITH

Born in Chicago, Illinois, the cradle of American architecture, the remarkable architect *Adrian Smith*, was influenced by the best and worked with them before founding his own office. He was a partner of SOM for more than four decades, and there he was commissioned to carry out wonders like the Burj Khalifa in Dubai, the Jin Mao tower in China, and the Trump International Hotel & Tower in Chicago.

When you go beyond fifty stories, the structural and mechanical
systems have to be rethought in terms of gravity and the
fact that at high altitudes the forces of the wind rule.

—ADRIAN SMITH

We return to the issue of the integration of a multidisciplinary team according to the project we are facing; no one is born knowing everything.

Today, with the coming of Industry 4.0, architects will not only have equipment but tools and systems that will lead us to create the future we dream of.

Building information modeling systems (BIMs) are a vital part of

TODAY, 4.0 ARCHITECTS WILL NOT ONLY HAVE EQUIPMENT BUT TOOLS AND SYSTEMS THAT WILL LEAD US TO CREATE THE FUTURE WE DREAM OF.

the construction industry, allowing everyone who is involved in the project to optimize and study the model carefully and thus make the best decision before starting the work. Recently, BIM has started to use artificial intelligence in its processes, allowing the improvement of these models that are adapted via machine learning, identifying patterns, and making independent improvement decisions. This is known as AI-assisted BIM.

As we see, we must adopt and understand these processes as quickly as possible, to adapt quickly to technological change and not only survive but transform ourselves along with it.

We are facing a changing world, and we must recognize that all this innovation and technology consume great resources. We must protect these resources as much as possible and guard against the inequities that will arise in society as resources grow scarcer.

> *The day that artificial intelligence is fully developed could spell the end of the human race. It will work by itself and redesign itself faster and faster. Human beings, limited by slow biological evolution, will not be able to compete with it and will be overcome.*
>
> **—STEPHEN HAWKING**

In times of profound social change (such as the COVID-19 pandemic global crisis), we must learn to adapt more than ever and learn the lessons that life is giving us. We have more than ever to learn that life is short and that one day we will no longer be here; that jobs are temporary because we depend on others, on circumstances, on the economy; that there is no greater wealth than health; today we have it, tomorrow who knows?; that we must appreciate who we have on our side, family, friends, companions, employees; that saving is important and buying more is not; that we should enjoy free time, which we have regularly; that we must exercise the mind to be strong, especially at times when someone else needs us; that it is important to know how to adapt and not settle; that we must learn to build new opportunities; and that everything happens as it unfolds and life is cyclical.

You cannot go back to correct mistakes. What matters in life are moments, emotions, memories. Today, once the lesson is learned, let's continue the march and try not to commit them again.

Surely some things will change as work and workplaces evolve. Many of our social habits changed during the pandemic, for example, including how we shop and whether we work five days a week in an office. It challenged the way we coexist within public spaces too, especially the closed and massive ones, such as transport stations, stadiums, concert halls … our urban space, which we will explore in our next chapter.

CHAPTER TEN

URBAN SPACES AND PLANNING

CHANCES FOR CHANGE

First we shape the cities—then they shape us.

—JAN GEHL

Urban planning is the set of disciplines in charge of the study, diagnosis, and design of human settlements—the urban planning of our cities.

Our cities must have urban spaces that reinvent themselves into places for all. For example, many town centers from Detroit to Monterrey, from Kolkata to Recife, are being abandoned both commercially and as places of residence. These places now have ridiculously low prices, and this is a great opportunity to turn them into unique projects like the one that I propose later.

We must take the concepts of a healthy city, green city, and zero-emission city, and create a more humane city that invites us to live together without taking health risks.

Since the modernist city of Brasilia, a planned city designed by Oscar Niemeyer and Lucio Costa or the planned city of Chandigarh in India, designed by Le Corbusier, we have not often ventured into building a city from scratch, until now with Masdar City appearing in Abu Dhabi.

For Zaha Hadid, the city must make us feel good, it must be an inclusive community, and it must solve both ecological and social challenges. For Cesar Pelli, this city should not be too big or neglect culture and education.

In short, let's hope in the first place to really implement solutions related to each citizen and their particular needs from the social and human point of view.

Urban Planning and Social Justice

There are many currents that tell us that we have to learn to do more with less ... I don't know, I don't think that after so much history, so much learning, and so much suffering, we should be so conformist.

In order to have a major change in all aspects of our life as society we must change some basic rules. Wouldn't we all love to live in a more equitable world without urban (and other forms of) poverty.

One of these systems we need to change is that we used to manage money that can be printed by powerful people that they lend to a world bank so that they in turn lend to central banks of each country, which in turn lend to local banks that transfer all the interest to the users. This definitely has to change. This system of economic slavery based on printed paper (and endlessly printing it) is ridiculous, and if we do not transform it into a more just system, we will not be able to take the next step that will, in turn, serve to have resources to transform our cities.

In 1971, in the term of US President Richard Nixon, it was decided to abandon the "gold standard." Prior to this, gold was the traditional world system in which basically a country established the value of its currency in relation to how much gold it owned. Then came the dollar and its monumental printers.

The truth is that the world economic system is no longer working, at least for the vast majority of nations and people. A reengineering of the capitalist system is urgently needed to make it fairer, and above all, now that AI will take hundreds of millions of jobs.

An idea that I share is universal basic income, which seems to become more appealing to some every day. It would be a type of social security system in which all citizens receive a sum of money monthly or receive services without conditions (it is not a credit; it does not have to be paid). This would make the right to housing, health, education, and food guaranteed to anyone in the world.

This system would transform the world as it would take more than a billion people who today have only one dollar a day to survive to be able to pay for services, housing, food, education, and health. It would transform half of the world population that lives on less than ten dollars a day. It would detonate the world economy extraordinarily.

Imagine that people no longer need to be exploited for their enormous need to eat and have shelter. Imagine children studying and playing; let's imagine a better world and fight for this change.

Money is only worthy because we determine its value. Let us make that role work for everyone, from a fair base, and from there, through personal effort, we achieve the well-being that each one desires. It is not about taking away from anyone, or lowering those above us, it is simply raising those below so that they can compete in equal circumstances.

Yes, this is a book about architecture and entrepreneurship, however, as entrepreneurs we need to change many social and economic rules in order to lend more opportunities for everybody. This will help us transform our urban spaces into safer, cleaner, more equitable environments.

IF YOUR DREAM IS TO BECOME AN ARCHITECT, THIS IS THE TIME.

Equal circumstances and opportunities for architects means we need to take advantage of local or international architecture competitions, no matter the size of our offices. These kinds of opportunities can represent a giant leap for our architectural practice.

We work in an interdisciplinary profession, no matter our scale, projects, or specialty. This is a spectacular profession and will be more and more challenging because the world is crowded, and the emerging economies will have a lot of new opportunities for us in the years to come—as well as problems to solve. *If your dream is to become an architect, this is the time.*

As we achieve a more balanced world, let's review the trends and projects that are already doing their part. From media libraries in Japan to hospitals in rural areas of Africa, these are some projects that are defining the new millennium around the globe.

With the intention of designing a cultural media center, the Sendai Media Library by Toyo Ito is innovative in both its engineering and aesthetics. This project is reminiscent of the Barcelona pavilion by Mies van der Rohe and Le Corbusier's Citrohan house, combining a set of slabs, structure, and the transparency of glass, achieving an open and fluid space. The structural solution based on transparent and moving "skeleton" columns is extraordinary—a game changer.

In a time in which libraries seemed to be disappearing, at least in terms of use and enjoyment by people, as well as funding, an excellent project by OMA, the Seattle Central Library, came to innovate the concept, transforming it into a civic space for all kinds of knowledge. Conceptualized by Rem Koolhaas and Joshua Prince-Ramus, the project travels in five horizontal planes in a movement that shapes its outer skin, faceted in transparent and translucent diamonds that reveal both the inner and outer world.

Described as an architecture or magic box adventure, the Phaeno Science Center in Wolfsburg, Germany, by the talented firm of Zaha Hadid Architects, continues the deconstructivism vision of this firm by creating complex, dynamic, and fluid spaces through undulated artificial hills and shaped valleys through daring spaces in movements that are now possible thanks to the advancement of structural and mechanical engineering, as well as innovative materials.

Another wonderful urban integration project aspires to provide greenspace like the famed Central Park in New York City. I'm referring to the High Line, which was born as a collaboration project of several architects, for a competition launched in 2003 that sought to renew the disused above-ground train tracks and invited architects to present innovative and daring projects. This is a 2.33 kilometer linear park in Manhattan. It uses an elevated section of the East Side line, inspired by the Coulée Verte René-Dumont in Paris, a similar 4.7 kilometer project completed in 1993. The High Line is conceived as an elevated green walkway that aims to refresh the city as it unfolds within it.

A wonderful and simple project designed to employ, educate, and empower a community, the Butaro Hospital was developed in Rwanda in 2011, in the district of Burera, which had a population of approximately three hundred forty thousand inhabitants and did not have a hospital. The Butaro Hospital developed by the MASS Design

Group was born. This project incorporates a variant of innovative elements designed to minimize the risk of infection. Interior hallways were removed, and large ceiling fans were installed, as well as louver windows, all to ensure air exchange and clean interior air. It also has UV light to kill or disable microbes. A continuous floor finish was also used to remove joints, prevent bacteria growth, and facilitate cleaning. Here, the concept of doing more with less is applied, using 100 percent local people for its construction and utilizing materials from the region.

Another excellent project that is remarkably integrated into the surrounding urban planning is Emerson College Los Angeles Center, designed by Morphosis. This building is made up of two residential towers for more than two hundred students, bridged by a ten-level multipurpose building that encloses a central space as an external courtyard, defined by multilevel terraces for the integration of its students, and all this shaded by a corrugated exterior membrane that covers the interior façades of the building.

Designed with the LEED Gold level certification in mind, this new center demonstrates its commitment to sustainability and responsibility to its community.

Don't Stand Still

In Africa, every morning when the sun rises, the gazelle knows that it has to run faster than the others to avoid being eaten. In Africa, every morning when the sun rises, the lion knows that it has to run faster than the slowest gazelle to avoid starvation.

It doesn't matter if you are the gazelle or the lion ... when the sun rises, you better start running.

This African proverb is deeply instructive about life, as it really reflects from the point of view of the *self*. The individual who alone finds their internal strength that awakens a drive in them and forces them to get ahead every day, to move, to not be still, to not let himself or herself be defeated, to discover that every day offers new opportunities and that every time we fall asleep, we die to wake up to life the next day and start again.

> **IT DOESN'T MATTER IF YOU ARE THE GAZELLE OR THE LION ... WHEN THE SUN RISES, YOU BETTER START RUNNING.**

And this is the world of companies, be they architectural firms or the bakery on the corner, or even Apple. We cannot stand still. Companies that do not move, that are not growing ... are dying, slowly, one by one, like the gazelle that waits for the lion to pass by. Costs rise and profits decrease, customers go to the next business.

It does not matter if our company is a family business, or a Fortune 500 global corporation, we must have a solid product, a growth strategy, and not allow ourselves to stand still. We must become as much as possible the "ink of our industry;" we must be that office that all turn to see. If we are not, we must have the courage to change to pursue that goal.

But uncontrolled growth can also lead us to disappear, it is important to maintain an adequate size whereby the promise of our brand does not disappear. Sometimes we grow so large that we lose control of what is happening around us, and customers no longer receive what they previously received directly from us.

That is why it is important to:

- Pay attention to the earnings, to be able to have enough flow to reinvest and save for the next business disruption

- Maintain an infrastructure that allows us to control the quality of what we offer to customers
- Learn what is important to our business and what is not
- Know what risks exist for our business and industry, and have a plan for each type of risk
- Have adequate cash flow for the cycles of our business

Architecture, unlike many other professions, does not require us to create such a large company in order to stand out, since many prestigious and award-winning colleagues develop their profession from small trenches.

The Pritzker

A smart way to stand out is through constant participation in architecture competitions as I said before. The pinnacle of worldwide recognition in the world of architecture is undoubtedly obtaining the prestigious Pritzker Prize.

In the mid-1970s, this award was a vision of the then-director of the National Arts Foundation, Robert Carleton Smith, who believed in the need to promote a project that would reward the most outstanding architects of the moment.

This award, sponsored since 1979 by Jay and Cindy Pritzker (Hyatt Foundation), is presented to an architect or group of architects whose work combines qualities of talent, vision, and commitment, and who have produced consistent and valuable works for their community and environment.

As proof of this, I present here a brief review of some of its winners.

The first to obtain this honor was the architect Philip Johnson in 1979, in recognition of his trajectory and his life achievements, as well as the multiple projects embodied for the benefit not only of his clients but also of the communities where they were built. One of his most representative works is the Glass House (1949).

In 1980, the Mexican Luis Barragán was honored for his commitment to architecture as a sublime act of the poetic imagination. Barragán is an example who demonstrates that it is not necessary to have a large company to achieve being an extraordinary architect. His works include the Luis Barragán house and the Faro del Comercio in Monterrey, and the monumental sculpture complex, Torres de Satélite.

I am fully aware, therefore, that the prize awarded to me is an act of recognition of the universality of culture and in particular of the culture of my homeland. But since nobody ever owes everything to himself, it would be mean to not remember at this time the collaboration, help and encouragement that I have received throughout my life from colleagues, cartoonists, photographers, writers, journalists and personal friends. Who have been kind enough to take an interest in my work.

—LUIS BARRAGÁN, PART OF HIS SPEECH WHEN ACCEPTING THE PRITZKER PRIZE IN 1980

In 1983, I. M. Pei received the award, an extraordinary Chinese-American architect who has brought architecture some of its most beautiful interior spaces and exterior forms. Proof of this was the remodeling of the Louvre museum, with its famous pyramid.

In 1988, Oscar Niemeyer was awarded this prestigious recognition. From his first works to the design and creation of the new capital Brasilia, Niemeyer shaped today's Brazil. He has captured the essence of his country and transformed it into extraordinary projects. Among them, the Museum of Contemporary Art of Niteroi, Brasilia, and its buildings stand out. He also participated in the team that created the United Nations Secretariat building in New York with Le Corbusier.

Leading in Architecture

Leadership is an example for the world of architecture and an incentive for thousands of colleagues and students of this wonderful profession, so become the leader your town or country needs.

These leaders (like those listed in the previous section) needed to create organizations with a superior spirit and quality, properly choose their collaborators and inject discipline and responsibility, and complement them via training but above all, by example.

Life is full of opportunities, those that we had and let go, those that we have and have not known how to recognize, and those that will come if we are awake so as to not let them pass again.

As my father said, "Do not regret what you did, repent what you did not do," that opportunity that you did not dare to take.

The best source of learning and the best competitive advantage that organizations have is the ability to learn quickly and much faster than their competitors, especially now in this changing world. What was a hit just six months ago no longer is today.

In order to lead by example, we must first find that inner voice, the one that motivates and moves us, and so we can teach others to find their own voice. We must learn to yield rather than demand, to suppress our own interests until we understand those of others and thus foster win-win relationships.

We must work on our emotional intelligence, that ability to communicate effectively with others, to have social sensitivity, empathy, the ability to recognize our weaknesses and strengths, and above all the ability to master our emotions and understand those of others.

If we analyze our behavior, many decisions we make in our daily lives are influenced by emotions. Do you remember impulsive decisions you made or times you lost your temper over something that was not terribly important?

Count to twenty and react after that.

In the future we may work in a more collaborative international environment, contributing our ideas and expertise to larger companies or perhaps to other governments or institutions, all this without the need to be out of our homes as technology allows us to be almost omnipresent. These collaborative situations will include strategic thinking or consultation analysis. Companies worldwide can reap benefits from our experience, and so it's time to incorporate many of these services and start to spread the word about us. The internet is here to help do the marketing for us.

> **LET'S NOT LOSE SIGHT OF OUR OWN MISSION; LET'S NOT LOSE THAT GOAL THAT IS REACHED STEP BY STEP.**

It seems that architects have always been born with the need to transcend through our works. It is an obsession that haunts us from the first projects in our university training, and that need is gasoline for this engine that we carry inside, which is revolutionized day by day and project by project. Let's not lose sight of our own mission; let's not lose that goal that is reached step by step. When you least feel it, you will already be at the next level, and your soul will speak through iron, cement, and glass.

Our profession, the most beautiful in the world, modesty aside, allows us to do wonderful things for the client, the community, and our cities and urban places, but despite having extraordinary architects and amazing projects, I think we have neglected urbanism. Our cities are not on par with our individual architecture, and there is a great opportunity there. It is not only about creating new cities but rather about redesigning the current cities to recycle and return to green and spacious spaces for outdoor recreation, leaving the car and transforming these spaces into parks and areas for cultivation or sports.

CHAPTER ELEVEN

THE FUTURE AWAITS

PREDICTING ARCHITECTURE'S WORLD

When you make a choice, you change the future.

—DEEPAK CHOPRA

The best way to predict the future is to create it, and for that we must be active participants in change and not just spectators. That is one of the greatest risks that our society faces. We all complain bitterly about various problems, but few of us do anything to change it. We know of our personal shortcomings, but many of us do nothing to improve ourselves.

We have become a comfortable society, and few are committed to exploring their own ideas and creating change.

I also see a divided society. Yes, with many good intentions and efforts across multiple organizations, groups, individuals, and companies, but each pulling in their own direction. In the last decades, we have been lacking authentic leadership of that amalgam that makes us all row together, in unison.

And this has opened the door for pseudo leaders, for characters who only seek their own benefit.

As we mature and achieve changes as a society in economic and political systems, as well as human rights and equality, let us do a thinking exercise and analyze how we can improve our cities of the future through responsible urbanism for the benefit of humanity.

If we look at today, we have megalithic urban centers, many very poorly organized and/or without analytical urban planning, not well executed and operated. Half of the world's population already lives in them, and this figure will reach at least 65 percent by 2050.

Our first priority must be sustainability, not only economic but also in terms of food and water, in addition to the treatment and recycling of all types of waste.

Solar and wind energy, urban gardens, and autonomous driving are and will be increasingly visible in our cities. This includes the limited use of cars in certain areas of the city and the notable improvements in public electric transport, as well as large pedestrian or transport areas in bicycle or personal mini-vehicles such as electric scooters.

These kinds of transformations are already happening and will keep guiding changes for the next decade or two, in addition to the automation of our cities supported by Big Data systems.

Only those who are building the future
have the right to judge the past.

—FRIEDRICH NIETZSCHE

Songdo, South Korea

The Songdo International Business District, still being built after over two decades and currently with more than one hundred thousand inhabitants, is trying to be one of the world's first "smart" and totally sustainable cities.

The city has 40 percent of its urban area covered by green areas, is totally wireless, and has sensors to control traffic and the environment. It has pneumatic tube systems that are responsible for making garbage disappear (where it is sorted and recycled), and the majority of its buildings are expected to recycle a large percent of the water they use, as well as include the use of renewable energy.

One of its main problems has been convincing companies and people to move to the new city, very similarly to what happened in Brasilia in its time. Six hundred hectares had to be reclaimed from the sea for construction. This land "won" from the sea is not the right thing, in my opinion. We must redesign our new cities without taking more of nature's territory; we must also recycle the land within the cities.

As we see, there are multiple factors that intervene in the success of a new city, but as always, the cost of individual property restrains some.

On the other hand, too, creating a totally new city turns some of its spaces into poorly copied other cities, since they do not have the flavor that occurs when inhabitants imprint on their cities as they develop.

When you visit these cities, like in the case of Dubai, you will be amazed by their buildings and some developed areas. However, for the most part, the city is cold with no unique flavor beyond its impressive new buildings. It has small areas of great design, but a poorly designed layout, if we're talking about the urban landscape.

We must design our cities with different measurements of success and uses, such as agricultural and food production areas. Large towns and cities must be fewer than a hundred kilometers from so-called

WE MUST DESIGN OUR CITIES WITH DIFFERENT MEASUREMENTS OF SUCCESS AND USES, SUCH AS AGRICULTURAL AND FOOD PRODUCTION AREAS.

"mega cities," to facilitate the daily transport of produce, and to also avoid dependence on foreign supplies as much as possible and regional conflicts that interfere with supplies or make their marketing more expensive.

There will also be cities with an industrial vocation, mainly reimagined to be able to produce a total under-ground infrastructure with 90 percent automation without humans, without atmospheric pollution, and without invading lands that would be better reclaimed for natural vegetation, recovering forests, and fauna.

These types of "factory" cities could be in desert lands but underground, beyond the "Natural Regenerable Zone" (NRZ), or that area in which the ecosystem of each region needs to self-regenerate. This includes the aquifers; that way we could migrate all our factories below ground.

Singapore

The history of this city dates back to the second century AD, and modern Singapore started in 1819 when the English settled there. It was then occupied by the Japanese during the Second World War and became independent from the United Kingdom in 1963.

In order to cope with unemployment and a serious housing crisis, it started an ambitious modernization program that continues to this day. This combination of a city with history, and at the same time, ultramodern innovation, gives cities and their inhabitants a special identity.

Today, it has fast transport and is moving forward with a program to become less dependent on cars every day, all the while having 3D sensors that monitor the energy efficiency of its buildings. As for green architecture, they created *super trees* that regulate the temperature of the city, absorbing and dispersing heat, in addition to collecting rainwater. They also have the largest green vertical residential area in the world, called the Tree House.

> *Decaying men and people live by remembering where they come from ... Great men and strong people just need to know where they are going.*
>
> **—JOSÉ INGENIEROS**

Copenhagen, Denmark

The Danish capital is undoubtedly one more example of history and modernity, as well as being one of the most technological cities in the world, but with the characteristic of being a "receptive city," since it puts its citizens at the center of the action by considering them in its design. Citizens, in turn, are very participatory in its design by sharing data that helps optimize the city. A receptive city puts the citizen at the center, giving them an active role and the power to be participative members of their communities.

It is also a cyclist's paradise, and it plans to neutralize its carbon footprint by 2025, as well as achieving fossil fuel independence by 2050.

To be classified as a smart city, our cities must have at least these four points:

1. Energy efficiency and environmental care
2. Efficient communication between its citizens, institutions, and companies
3. Sharing goods and services and integration with all information technologies
4. Communication and robotics

Smart cities must promote a sustainable lifestyle, and this should be reflected, depending on the identity of each town, in its culture, customs, and above all, the self-determination of its citizens and not their governments.

The future should also have more hours of leisure and reduced working hours. For this there are already several propositions, from Fridays off to the "four-hour week." Whatever it is, we citizens must participate more with our cities and need more time to do so. We should encourage the existence of "collaborating citizens" programs through which we can sign up to contribute our time to noble causes for the betterment of our cities. This type of individual contribution will unify social groups and give us the awareness that we lack today, since the vast majority of us are oblivious to the solutions or even to the problems of our communities. We are merely entities that wander within it, absorbed in our own problems and daily routines.

Both architecture (for the individual) and urbanism (for the community) are at the service of humanity, and today's cities, based on old traces from their origin, have not been renewed. Instead, they are just a collage of ideas without connection and planned with large spaces for private transport.

The Line

The Line in Saudi Arabia, which has broken ground, sounds like something out of science fiction. Planned as a linear city, it will have a massive wall over a hundred miles long. The city will be powered by renewable, sustainable, green energy. Transportation and infrastructure will be underground. The latest AI will monitor data, try to be predictive, and attempt to make the city operate as efficiently as possible for its intended nine million inhabitants. It will have modules that, according to its creators, will allow you to walk to all services and activities in less than five minutes. It aims to have a carbon footprint of only 2 percent compared to current modern cities.

This type of supposedly cutting-edge project, in my opinion, will be an example of misunderstood urban planning. I predict a resounding failure since cities cannot be created and adapted to human use by force. It remains to be seen if those nine million will arrive or even adapt to it.

Cities throughout history have been growing as their inhabitants grow, and it is the needs and visions of citizens that lead cities to be what they are today and what they'll be tomorrow.

CHAPTER TWELVE

PAST TO PRESENT TO ...?

FROM BEING NOMADS TO BEING SEDENTARY TO BECOMING NOMADS AGAIN

Only when love takes the lead will the earth, and life on earth, be safe again. And not until then.

— LEWIS MUMFORD

Where are we going in the future? The far future? We no longer will inhabit the same locality throughout our lives, we will move and work from all corners of the world ... and then outside of the blue marble.

The immediate future is already here, but what is my vision of what cities will be like beyond 2050?

As we move forward, we develop, and above all, learn. We discover that instead of knowing more … we know less. Each door of knowledge that we open leads to others. The more we develop, we see how far we still have to go, and part of this paradigm leads us to visualize that we cannot continue living in a model of cities created in the Renaissance of the fifteenth century. Cities where the plaza is the center, leading to political and religious power on both sides.

These cities were governed initially for carts and carriages and now by and for the automobile. Instead, the essential element should be human beings within biodiversity, respecting the surrounding environment; that is the axis on which we must build the city of the future.

EACH DOOR OF KNOWLEDGE THAT WE OPEN LEADS TO OTHERS. I don't pretend to imagine the technological future. I already take for granted that right now thousands of minds and companies are working on what our technological future will be, and it will probably change every five years, opening more doors as it progresses.

In the same way, I take for granted that buildings in new or reimagined cities will generally and specifically feature advances in ecotechnology, LEED regulation, telecommunications, smart mobility, energy and recycling management, security, and smart public services. All this duly analyzed and optimized by Big Data systems.

Regarding technological advances, I am concerned that the solutions of all kinds that we develop for any problem do not consider the total environment. What will we be damaging without realizing it?

The past, the present, and the future are about us, human beings, and about the ecosystem we have—everything else is just accessories.

And on the Seventh Day, God Rested ...

The first human beings formed in small groups and were *nomads*.

They needed to move from one place to another in search of food, shelter, and to travel according to the seasons. Little by little, they learned to cultivate, and that led them to think about protecting their crops and staying close to them, as well as their sources of water, be it rivers or lakes. They then became *sedentary* (they settled), and thus the first human settlements were formed.

According to archaeological findings, the first settlements were around the year 10,000 before our era, between the Tigris and Euphrates rivers in the area known as Mesopotamia, or present-day Iraq.

The source of water and the possibility of harvesting led these small groups to adopt this new lifestyle. More free time led to a series of inventions and new activities determining the formation of primitive societies. This type of population multiplied in Egypt, China, India, and eventually in Meso- and South America.

Home, for the moment, is Earth, and there is only one, and we are undoubtedly the species responsible for it. We have done great damage to our planet from an ecological point of view. Global warming has led to climate change, which has led to amplified and more recurrent natural disasters like hurricanes and droughts. Add to that overexploitation of resources, deforestation, and pollution of all kinds, and we really became the invasive species. We are a type of cannibal. Even though we do not feed on our species' flesh, we kill each other in wars, nevertheless.

> THE PAST, THE PRESENT, AND THE FUTURE ARE ABOUT US, HUMAN BEINGS, AND ABOUT THE ECOSYSTEM WE HAVE— EVERYTHING ELSE IS JUST ACCESSORIES.

If this is the world that will continue, I don't think we have a long time to go.

All of this means we must find an accelerated solution to make amends to the planet for the damage we have caused it, to repair it, and to be more conscious with our fellow humans.

This leads me to remember a wonderful Nahuatl poem, attributed to Nezahualcóyotl, the "Poet King" of Texcoco, born in 1402 before the arrival of the Spanish in Mexico.

> *Nelia nikkinelia sensontle ikuika, Tototl tien setsontli*
> *itoskaj, Nelia nikiknelia nopa xoxoktetl, Uan*
> *nelia tlen kualtsin ininuajuiyaka xoxchimej, sanke*
> *notlakaiknin ya ika nochi noyoltsin nikiknelia.*
> *I love the song of the mockingbird,*
> *Bird of four hundred voices,*
> *I love the color of jade*
> *And the intoxicating scent of flowers,*
> *But more than all I love my brother, man.*[3]

In 1992, a group of Nobel Prize winners and more than seventeen hundred independent scientists, in conjunction with the Union of Concerned Scientists (UCS), published a "warning" document on the environmental impact of human activities. The term *climate change* had been coined, along with problems that we all already know, like the lack of fresh water, mass extinction of species, overexploitation of the sea, etc. Thirty years later very little but close to nothing has been done, and we are getting alarmingly worse at an exponential rate.

Climate change has been defined by the United Nations as "an existential threat to life on the planet." The private sector and non-

---

3   Accessed January 3, 2023, https://poetry.arizona.edu/blog/400-voices.

governmental organizations now have key roles in forcing govern-ments, and through them the population, to take immediate action, otherwise the planet itself will torment us. Today, the people of our planet are recovering from the pandemic ... tomorrow, who knows what the challenges will be?

We must then create more land and marine reserves, ban poaching and wildlife trade, change our diet to a more plant- and fruit-based diet, switch to renewable energy, and adopt green technologies. But above all, we must *reinvent our urban environment.*

The footprint of some cities, especially in developed countries like the United States, is enormous. Just take a look and see the size of any major city in the US via satellite. For example, take a look at Metro Atlanta (more than 5 million people/4,280 km^2/7.5 tons of CO_2 per person) and compare it, for example, with Barcelona (1.7 million people/162 km^2/0.7 ton of CO_2 per person).

One way to observe this is by flying from London to Mexico at night, when soaring over the US territory. It is impressive to see, by the lights of the cities that dominate, 90 percent of the land full of lights versus very few spots without light. And that's the way it is for four or five hours through the East Coast, until finally reaching Mexican territory, where the power goes out and the spectrum turns. Over Mexico you see 90 percent black spots and 10 percent city lights.

As I mentioned before, creating completely new cities, in addition to their cost and negative footprint in destroyed space, leads to the cost per housing unit being much higher than in existing cities.

This is not the solution.

Cities require identity, that which is achieved through the years and that people give to them. Cities full of life and with inhabitants already identified with their culture and idiosyncrasies are necessary, which is why I firmly believe that the future of our great cities is the regeneration of the cities that we already have.

Imagine that we condensed Atlanta or Mexico City or Jakarta without moving their location, and respecting their physical essence as much as possible, until we reduce their footprint to 30 percent of the space they currently have and returning the remaining 70 percent to:

1. Forests (biodiversity)
2. Spaces for food cultivation and solar or wind cultivation
3. Outdoor recreation and sport
4. Education and social integration centers

The 30 percent that would make up the preexisting urban spot would respect the most significant buildings in the metropolis, those which historically have given identity to the city, those should remain surrounded by natural parks and nature itself as the buildings that used to take up that space are recycled.

Investments would be made in low carbon technologies, new buildings would be reconfigured for mixed uses, and new mobility systems would be offered, including individual electric transport and public transport, also electric.

The condensation of this 30 percent would lead to two solutions, both vertical; taller and more efficient buildings combined with buildings that would be built downward. Yes, underground.

These new buildings could have, for example, 50 percent of their structure above ground and the other 50 percent below it.

The construction of these mega vertical buildings will respect the space that we call the "ground floor" today, designed for people, up to a height sufficient for the growth of surrounding trees. From there, perhaps fifteen or twenty meters above, the second, third, fourth, etc. levels will appear.

The part of the building that will be underground will respect the layer of soil that serves for the fertilization and maintenance of the topsoil and hydraulic regeneration in the same way, and the first negative levels (basement one, two, etc.) will appear after this area, perhaps thirty or forty meters lower and possibly reaching up to one hundred meters below ground. The vertical transport systems (elevators), will transport people between the levels in a matter of minutes or even seconds.

There are already examples of civilizations or urban spaces built underground, from Derinkuyu, Cappadocia, in Turkey, in buildings dating from the eighth century BC, to the Path of Toronto in Canada, which at almost thirty kilometers in length is considered the largest underground shopping complex in the world.

Hong Kong is betting on these types of solutions; it has been forced to do so due to the lack of space on its surface. The use of these spaces could free up to a thousand hectares of their current surface.

In New York, taking advantage of its unused railway tunnels, the Lowline was a project (at this point, a prototype), which will be the first underground park in the world. It will include a system that will allow sunlight to reach and maintain a mini forest, as well as ventilation and temperature maintenance technologies.

There are countless advantages to having part of our cities underground in addition to protecting from extreme climates. For example, in winter, that part of the city would need less energy to warm up, and in summer, less energy to cool off. In the case of housing, tornado disasters would not have to be endured each year, destroying thousands of homes not to mention human losses.

We would save on materials for the exterior since there would practically be no façades; underground construction, done correctly, would not harm the environment and the landscape. Of course, not all types of land are conducive to building underground; the type of soil and the depth of the construction will determine its viability.

In the deepest part of the constructions there would be large water tanks, with natural, recycled water, and rainwater. We would have inverted cones for ventilation, lighting, and rainwater harvesting.

Most of our activities that do not require continuous external contact or natural light could take place underground, for example, warehouses, factories, auditoriums, etc. In short, there are many human activities that we do today on the surface, being inside all the time and without use of windows or natural lighting, take factories for example, or storage spaces, or even theaters.

Another advantage is the lower impact of earthquakes. According to calculations, these constructions can reduce damage by up to a fifth.

We would protect ourselves from solar radiation. In addition, by having a stable temperature all year round, we could be less susceptible to seasonal diseases due to constant temperature changes.

Living underground would prepare humanity to take that great leap ... living in space.

I think beyond 2100, humanity will be divided between living on Earth, or rather below it, and in space in orbital stations around us, perhaps going down to vacation once a year or whenever possible, at that great natural park called *the blue planet.*

LIVING UNDERGROUND WOULD PREPARE HUMANITY TO TAKE THAT GREAT LEAP... LIVING IN SPACE.

Although not all cities will be candidates for this type of new urbanism, mainly due to their topographical and soil conditions, the vast majority will be. This new lifestyle will lead us to develop new technologies to be able to live in true carbon zero environments, and to reconnect with nature and fauna. In some places, animals took to the streets when we were sheltered at home during the pandemic, which was an interesting sight to see.

Multiple projects are already preparing us for underground buildings called "earth scrapers," as well as cities enabling urban master plans to connect and expand their cities underground, like Helsinki, which has a history of proposing these types of projects. This reinforces a new attitude of acceptance for this new type of urbanism.

Paris, Singapore, and many other cities are considering it too. In 2017, the city of Paris launched a competition to reinvent unused underground spaces. Singapore has even changed its laws so that underground space is also state land.

However, I faithfully believe that all extremes are dangerous, so to speak. Therefore, the solution is a combination of outside and inside, or in this case, up and down.

Nomads

The conditions of quarantine led us to accelerate processes and discover that the ways working will change significantly. Working in the same place and in the same company for years has largely disappeared as an employment model.

New jobs before AI takes over will be short term. This movement started some years ago, and this will lead us to be nomads again.

The nomads of the twenty-first century began in part thanks to the great internationalization of work and communications, in the form of transnational companies looking for and moving personnel from country to country. Then, the digital age expanded this work system even more and everything was catapulted by the pandemic, which revolutionized and verified the fact that we can work from our homes, in most cases without sacrificing productivity. Home today can be almost anywhere as long as there's access to the internet and, thanks to the advancement of technology, to the Starlink network. Once it is 100 percent functional, it will make it easier for us to live where we want or where that short-term contract may take us.

We are becoming digital nomads.

We will be constant travelers; we will get lost in the world to find ourselves. We will absorb cultures, we will understand our fellows, we will share their passion for what gives identity to their cities.

This new reality will lead us to never buy a house again but rather to rent. Rents are and will be the future of real estate investments. The costs of land will drop noticeably, especially when it comes to production activities. All the spaces that are today above ground and don't use windows will depend on artificial lighting and ventilation. Why waste square meters of green in areas that could easily be underground?

This will accelerate the creation of efficient transport systems both within and between cities. We will no longer need to buy cars; most of the old roads will be transformed into pedestrian, green spaces, and spaces for one-person personal transportation vehicles, perhaps the old skateboard already modernized.

Living underground will contribute to a return to the balance that this planet lost due to the exponential growth in cities that were also not planned or transformed for this enormous migration of people.

The current responsibility for our urban planning falls into the hands of the government, and we know that now and every day, more and more governments have demonstrated their inefficiency. This new model of cities should have regions with general rules but managed by private companies.

This new model will create investment funds that will be shares that individuals will buy instead of having or investing in a house, so we will be partners in urban growth. We will rent, but the assets of what we now call a house will be invested in large developments.

It is not only in number of beings that we populate and pollute the planet and its enormous atmosphere but also with our structures that, little by little, end forests, lakes, and seas.

As I said earlier, we saw with joy how during quarantine many animal species emerged again. Imagine what would happen if 70 percent of the footprint of our cities returned to them, the owners of the space before we became the dominant species. Imagine again bees pollinating, beavers building dams, rhinos running through the African grassland, without extinction.

Imagine being in an advanced vertical transport system and heading to the surface to eat, walk, or play tennis. You are transported from a completely different world, under the trees and under the ground, in a matter of seconds. The elevator slows down, the doors open, and you will be surprised again by the beauty of nature around you. See the blue sky again, free of pollution, see that your children can breathe without the need for devices, as many diseases may have been left behind.

Inside, technological systems with screens in our homes, instead of windows, would project the image that our minds want ... that favorite beach, that view from the last hotel we visited ... there are no limits, we will not feel that we are inside. And if we want to go outside, we will be an elevator ride away.

Reflection systems will allow the sun to peek in, filling the room with natural light and warmth.

And if we move to the indicated depth, perhaps we will also be protected from natural disasters, each more frequent thanks to our lack of responsibility with the ecosystem, and even possibly the fall of a meteorite without the need to evacuate since we would be in the ideal bunker.

The cities that I propose are the same current cities, but reimagined and reinvented, recovering a large percentage of semi-abandoned or underused property and generating large buildings that will have a balance between underground and aboveground vertical construction. These buildings will now consume 10 percent of the space used by their predecessor properties and the remaining 90 percent will rejoin the flora and fauna of that area.

With current technologies and with different examples of urban areas already underground, such as those that exist in Toronto (Path) and in different parts of the world that prove to us that we can live part of our lives underground, we will be able to build mega towers with perhaps 60 percent of their square meters underground.

Yes, the financial cost would be enormous, but as I said before, money is only paper printed by our controllers, those self-proclaimed pseudogods. When we realize that 99 percent is more than the 1 percent, we can achieve this and many more changes.

A new way to prove this is cryptocurrency, created by someone (just like paper money only now even without it) who got enough people to trust in his payment method without any backing other than that of its own users.

The followers are then those who give value to electronic money or paper money control systems; it is the number of people who use it and accept it that drives crypto, not if it has a real endorsement as the gold standard had previously.

Three thousand years into the future, humanity lives on earth completely under it, while its servant robots work on the surface reaping; another type of human, the space humans, live outside of earth, as well as on many other planets.

—ISAAC ASIMOV, *THE CAVES OF STEEL*

There is no longer a supreme authority that dictates the *what* and the *how*; governments lose more credibility day by day, and this is because the most inept or corrupt people, with the most thirst for power, slither as candidates into some political position and then sneak their other inept friends in to obtain complete control. Inept they may be but, at the same time, they are skilled in trying to convince us that they want an improvement for all, when in reality they are only looking for their own benefit.

> TO ACHIEVE THE CHANGE WE WANT IN OUR SOCIETY AND IN OUR FUTURE CITIES, WE MUST BE MUCH MORE PARTICIPATIVE AND ACHIEVE A REAL MERITOCRACY.

So, to achieve the change we want in our societies and in our future cities, we must be much more participative and achieve a real meritocracy, a system in which the most capable are really selected to participate in our democratic systems.

The word *meritocracy* comes from *meritum*, which means due reward, and *kratos*, which means power or strength … knowing how to choose the best based on merit.

Let us not be influenced by what Google learns or takes from us without our authorization, so that Amazon can offer us what it thinks we want or need, and then pretend that we are happy on Facebook. Those algorithms that assume our future are already on the way to being obsolete.

Let's go back to our basics: family, friends, and our inner self. To the beautiful and simple things in life, to see the sunrise every day, that little hummingbird that came to our window, or to enjoy the ants walking in line while they work collectively for the good of the colony. Let's start by knocking on the neighbor's door, introducing ourselves, and bringing them some homemade cookies.

> *The extension of the art of housing is the art of living,*
> *living in harmony with the deepest impulses of man*
> *and with his adopted or prefabricated environment.*

—CHARLOTTE PERRIAND

In the meantime, AI systems will transform life in our cities, companies like Nvidia and Microsoft CityNext, and many others are already working to help cities around the world to be more competitive, sustainable, and prosperous.

Predictive analytics will tell us where to park or if it is better to take the bus instead of taking the car, and to convince us, they will give us a discount on transportation and also perhaps offer our parking, which many will no longer use, at auction for someone who will use it within the city.

Before leaving home, we will know if there is a free court to play tennis and if the fourth for doubles has committed or not.

This reminds me of a joke my father told me (my doubles partner for many years). Once two tennis players wondered if there would be tennis courts in the afterlife, and they swore an oath; the first to die would return to tell the other if there were or not. Years later, one of them dies, and after three days he returns to tell his friend who is still alive.

"Edgard, I have news for you, one good and one bad, which do you want first?"

"The good one."

"There are tennis courts in heaven."

"And the bad one?"

"We have a game next Sunday."

Well, perhaps analytical data prediction will also tell us this someday.

As the world turns and technology advances, let us remember that the change is in us, that achieving that goal is in us, that starting to move is in us, that reaching that best position, that best project, is only in us, in pushing more than others and not letting ourselves be defeated.

If you move, you live, but if you move faster and before anyone else, you live better.

The nail holds the horseshoe, the horseshoe the horse,
the horse the man, and the man … the universe.

—ARABIC PROVERB

Under the Sea

Well, the future of our cities will not ignore our oceans. Three quarters of our planet are covered by them, after all. If we will already be living underground, why not under the sea?

"There it is, Venice, the opulent owner of ancient, noble, and free coats of arms, Venice the beautiful, the village that counts. That the ground has magnificent nations … lady of the sea," as José Zorrilla's poem goes.

The magic and romanticism of Venice, with its navigable paths and openness to all seas has awakened many ideas, and perhaps inspired by it, surprising projects have been developed.

A floating city for up to ten thousand inhabitants and part of the United Nations program to improve the urban future is being planned. This proposal of the firm OCEANIX considers a self-sufficient city, capable of resisting natural disasters (well, there is no need to challenge nature; we have already seen what happened to the *Titanic*) and made up of a series of hexagonal platforms anchored to the ocean floor, creating a sustainable artificial ecosystem that will channel the flows of energy, water, food, and waste to create a modular maritime metropolis.

NINE OUT OF TEN OF THE LARGEST CITIES IN THE WORLD THAT ARE CURRENTLY ADJACENT TO THE SEA WILL SUFFER FROM INCLEMENT CLIMATE CHANGE.

Nine out of ten of the largest cities in the world that are currently adjacent to the sea will suffer from inclement climate change, which will cause sea levels to rise perhaps more than three meters before 2050.

Whatever the destiny of our cities may be, it is important that we no longer affect the environment in a negative way. I think projects like OCEANIX are very valuable for our development, but I am concerned that we see this as the only solution.

We already have an extremely polluted ocean; we need no further proof than the floating plastic "cities" that we have created in the Pacific. The largest of these floating garbage patches is 1.6 square kilometers! Yes, I believe that the UN habitat program should first seek to clean this problem up before seeking to promote an ocean invasion. The existence of this plastic stain in the sea dates back to 1988 and yes, it continues to grow.

Climate Change Challenges

The UN Climate Change Conference, COP27, concluded in November 2022. It brought together over thirty-five thousand stakeholders, political leaders, civil society members, and other observers from 190 countries to find agreement on climate-related topics, including climate change adaptation, climate finance, decarbonization, agriculture, and biodiversity.

I hope COP28 includes urban planning and the transformation of cities that today represent almost 50 percent of human concentration and are responsible for the greatest pollution ever created by man.

Cities are key factors in addressing the climate challenges of the future, and not only this, we need changes to achieve the highest emotional well-being of their inhabitants through friendlier cities. Imagine 7 *billion* people living in cities by 2050. Currently, scientists have already detected a growing number of mental disorders due to life in cities. If we do not urgently transform design, the panorama of social stability looks very frightening.

Architecture is the will of an era translated into space.

—LUDWIG MIES VAN DER ROHE

And what will our life as a society in these times be like? Perhaps abrupt changes and a lot of spiritual solitude, continual crises, not to mention leaders who do not lead (or care), and unprecedented social unrest.

Do we really want this to be our children's inheritance? Are we going to leave them an inheritance of the task of amending our disasters? Or are we going to contribute our grain of sand individually and collectively to leave them a better future?

Every effort counts; we are the sum of individual efforts. We are the *architects* of our own destiny.

As we stop depending on our corrupt governments and start being much more participatory and demanding toward them, we will be able to forge a better world. We will not achieve anything trapped in the screen of our cell phones.

Vertical versus Horizontal

The buildings of the future, those that will transform the horizontal city and turn it into a vertical one below and above ground, will be able to rescue a large part of the urban sprawl, transforming it into green areas for agricultural production for self-supply and even recreational areas. From my point of view, this will significantly contribute to eradicating pollution by allowing mass vertical circulation to replace the car as the fundamental urban transport method.

These points can achieve a real transformation of our cities:

1. Transform deciduous and low-value urban sprawl (up to 85 percent in most cities) into complexes of buildings above and below ground.

2. Buildings from fifty thousand users living and working at an elevator distance, pedestrian communication between complexes or via electric trains above the level of the treetops in the area. The ground floors of each complex will be reserved 80 percent for the coexistence of people in an open covered area that does not obstruct circulation.

3. Eliminate urban vehicular traffic in these cities by 95 percent, transforming it into green areas and/or returning it to its origins: clean and flowing streams, community farmland, sports and leisure areas, among others.

4. Use of AI technologies for the optimal management of energy, waste, and use of facilities according to the needs of its users.

Our populations, already transformed into city nomads, will be travelers between cities, motivated to learn new cultures and strengthen global friendships. All this despite the current trend of emigrating from the countryside to the city, which will continue until it stabilizes due to the logic of the importance of agricultural production.

These new city dwellers will travel between cities, and they will no longer be more than three to five years in each one since we will be citizens of the globe.

A vital factor for our future will be education, since this will help our knowledge gradually become more equal and we will not have second-class citizens, culturally speaking. This will contribute even more to achieving common goals and having common projects, to the benefit of all and not just a few.

These more-educated citizens will be able to travel with short-term contracts around the planet, connecting from wherever they may be to their work meetings.

Socially we will share more. We will compete, yes, but in formal or informal sports, in those street games, but we will no longer compete so aggressively in political issues since with more education we will understand: first my community and then me. Of course, the more capable will obtain better results, but at least that will depend on each person and not on who drew the short stick of opportunities.

There will continue to be social classes, but we must aim for the poorest or lower-middle classes to disappear completely. It is not about taking away from those who duly and under their effort and intelligence managed to stand out and even accumulate wealth, but rather about giving back to those who are exploited. We must provide real opportunities so that everyone has the required levels of sufficiency in health, housing, food, education, and recreation.

Perhaps you have seen this demonstrated on a YouTube video. Let's imagine a five thousand-meter-long athletic track where ten runners with different economic backgrounds are about to compete. Instead of all standing at the starting line, due to their economic differences, many of which come from birth, some are standing ten, fifty, or maybe a thousand meters ahead, but even worse, others are not at the starting line, but behind it, possibly even up to two hundred meters behind. Will this be a fair competition? I think not.

Cities are one of the biggest contributors to global warming and climate change. In order not to reach a 1.5 degree increase in average temperatures, a rapid and far-reaching transformation will be required in the use of energy, urban spaces, and infrastructure, including means of transport and buildings as well as industrial systems.

The WHO stated that 93 percent of the world's children breathe polluted air every day, putting their health and development in serious danger. It is estimated that six hundred thousand children died from respiratory problems caused by pollution in their cities in the year 2016 alone.

We are going to continue losing the most valuable thing we have: our children, our futures, and all due to not wanting to transform our way of life and our polluting processes, many of them taking place within our cities. We are going to continue to regret doing nothing on the pretext of not having resources; we are going to continue assuming that we do not have economic resources because we do not want to transform our economic system based on control and exploitation without backing (even the claim that they are backed by gold is no longer true and was never fair to begin with, as most of that gold was stolen). The only backing that they have is their military power and a system so rotten and so ambitious that it only corrupts and exploits.

The simplest way to be happy is to do good.

—HELEN KELLER

Challenges such as the high energy consumption of the buildings of the future will be channeled through digitization and automation thanks to new architectural technologies, which will focus on increasing energy efficiency but also on transforming an urban sprawl into a large building or a set of buildings. We will be able to recycle the energy of that number of houses or independent units in this way and even recycle the waste in distributed energy loss by concentrating it in one or several megabuildings.

CHALLENGES SUCH AS HIGH ENERGY CONSUMPTION OF THE BUILDINGS OF THE FUTURE WILL BE CHANNELED THROUGH DIGITIZATION AND AUTOMATION.

The main objective of this type of building will be to achieve maximum energy efficiency and take advantage of renewable energies, for example air, through mini wind fans that can be distributed through the façades of these buildings, due to their great heights and structural systems.

Take the project by MAD architects in Quzhou, China, which is a concrete stadium buried in the ground and covered with grass on its roof, and which will have more than seven hundred thousand square meters of construction. Being conceived to be the largest underground shelter in the world, this project breaks the traditional design of sports center architecture.

There are already several world projects that seek to build underground. The truth is I am a great promoter of this type of project and of recovering land and resources for the forests, the jungle, or the savannah—what was theirs and that of the species that lived inside.

We are very, very small, but we are profoundly
capable of very, very big things.

—STEPHEN HAWKING

Whether in Milan, Singapore, Mexico, or São Paulo, urban parks, gardens, and orchards have multiplied on rooftops or outside of them, contributing little by little to mitigating the effects of greenhouse gases, since 70 percent of them are generated within cities.

Singapore, with its "super trees" zones, is a prime example of what can be achieved in the future in terms of returning the green to our cities. Under their immense greenhouses, they house botanical gardens with multiple species of plants from all continents.

Milan, with its vertical forest, is another example. Full of larches, cherry trees, apple trees, olive trees, and beech trees, each duly located and planted according to its resistance to wind and growth conditions, sun, and humidity.

Mexico City with its wonderful Bosque de Chapultepec contributes some to mitigate the enormous urban sprawl. In the past, there was an exemplary farming system used by the Mexicas to expand their territory in lakes and lagoons of the Valley of Mexico and in which they grew flowers and vegetables; they allow for the conservation of the lacustrine areas that are complex ecosystems with beneficial effects on the climate, air quality, and fish production.

Around 1265, the Aztec civilization had food shortages, so Tlatoani Acatonalli proposed to the council of elders a technique consisting of reclaiming land from the lake with floating fillings of silt and sticks. This is how the first chinampas were born to produce corn and various crops, guaranteeing the survival of our ancestors.

The agricultural system of the chinampas stands out for having a great biodiversity with fifty-one agricultural species. It is also home to 2 percent of world biodiversity and 11 percent of the national biodiversity with 139 species of vertebrates: twenty-one of them fish, six amphibians, ten reptiles, seventy-nine varieties of birds, and twenty-three species of mammals.

We have many ancient or recent examples, but it is the transmission of culture and education that will achieve a transformation in the mentality of our populations. The more knowledge we have, the less fear we will have; we will see that our communities are more important, and

COMMON WELFARE ALLOWS FOR A GREATER INDIVIDUAL BENEFIT.

putting them first is more beneficial than thinking only of our own well-being. Common welfare allows for a greater individual benefit.

Architecture is the great visual and collective contributor to our cultures and the intelligence of our people. That is the architecture that is here to stay, and that will be the new urbanism that will come to transform our society.

MY CREED

1. I firmly believe that the future of our cities lies in restructuring them and reducing the footprint of each one, building a large part underground, and at the same time, reaching unimaginable heights, reintegrating that soil into the nature to which it belongs.

2. I think that society will become nomadic again, leading us to share more than just space—instead, embracing culture and global identity.

3. I think we must correct our course before taking one more square meter of our forests and seas. There is so much urban landscape to be regenerated that it would be irresponsible to keep destroying green areas to grow uncontrollably and without proper planning.

4. I think that climate change will begin to correct itself from home, from the individual to the general, and this will be achieved through education, through the transformation of our educational models, but above all through leading by example, both individual and collective.

5. I believe that education and example are the greatest goods that we can inherit.

6. I believe in the human talent to create and conceive new, self-repairing, and printable materials that will allow us to preserve our nature in the most intact way possible.

7. I believe that our economic model must be restructured, have a basis for all via universal income, and from there each one can stand out based on effort and honest work.

8. I think that our democracy must also change and walk as far as possible toward a meritocracy. We are immersed in innumerable problems due to rulers who rule only to their advantage and not that of their communities. But those responsible are we who do not participate and we who allow the worst to rise to power.

9. I think we must change our interior in order to try to change the exterior. Change will come from the inside out, from the individual to the particular, but for that we must free our minds; that freedom comes from the peace of mind that our families have the necessary well-being and maximum opportunities and possibility.

10. I believe that the future city will not only be intelligent but will also operate as a large interconnected system based on instant data.

11. I believe that architecture will always be at the service of man and that it will continue to be a fundamental part of our society, and our work as architects will be complemented by AI systems.

12. I believe that disruptive technologies will empower us, and together with them we can evolve toward a better, fairer, and above all, more humane future.

13. I believe that as soon as we master all these points, we will be ready to live in space, on the nearby moons, and we will be able to turn Mars into our second Earth.

But before all this, we must transform our mentality, recognize ourselves as complementary individuals, extend our hand to those in need, but above all, demand the change of our authorities to achieve a meritocratic model.

I hope that the new urbanism contributes significantly to human well-being, and that as nomads of the globe, we unite as siblings who share the only current inhabitable home, this wonderful and blessed planet Earth.

AUTHOR'S NOTE

I hope that this first book in which I try to describe how talented and brilliant we are as architects, and the mix of entrepreneurs we have to be in order to succeed, has succeeded in awakening your interest to go one step further.

The next book in this trilogy will no longer deal with who we architects are and what we need to do to transcend in our professions, but it will deal entirely in the new urbanism I propose and what we must do to transform our life systems to achieve these new types of cities.

The last book will show the new urbanism based on five preselected cities around the world, and how to prepare our humanity to live outside our planet.

So what are you going to do now?

To improve yourself and to support real change.

A path is made by walking.

ACKNOWLEDGMENTS

In life we are passengers on the same bus. Someone gets on and someone gets off, but during the journey, we have the opportunity to meet extraordinary people. Many of them make our lives a little better; for all of you who know that you built my life and my apprenticeship, I thank you deeply with all my heart.

I hope I have touched your life for the better, even if only briefly.

GET IN TOUCH

www.cearcarquitectura.com

www.edgardrios.com

e.rios@cearcarquitectura.com

Facebook/Instagram: @cearc.arquitectura

Printed in the USA
CPSIA information can be obtained
at www.ICGtesting.com
JSHW082349140824
68134JS00020B/1972